DR FRANKENSTEIN'S
HUMAN BODY
BOOK

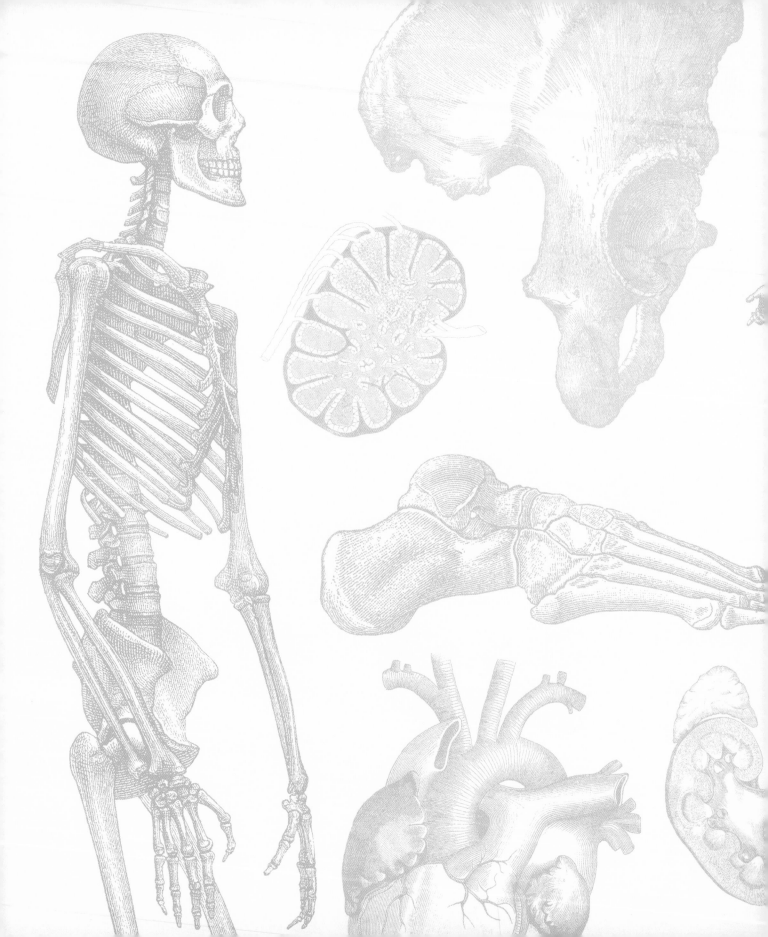

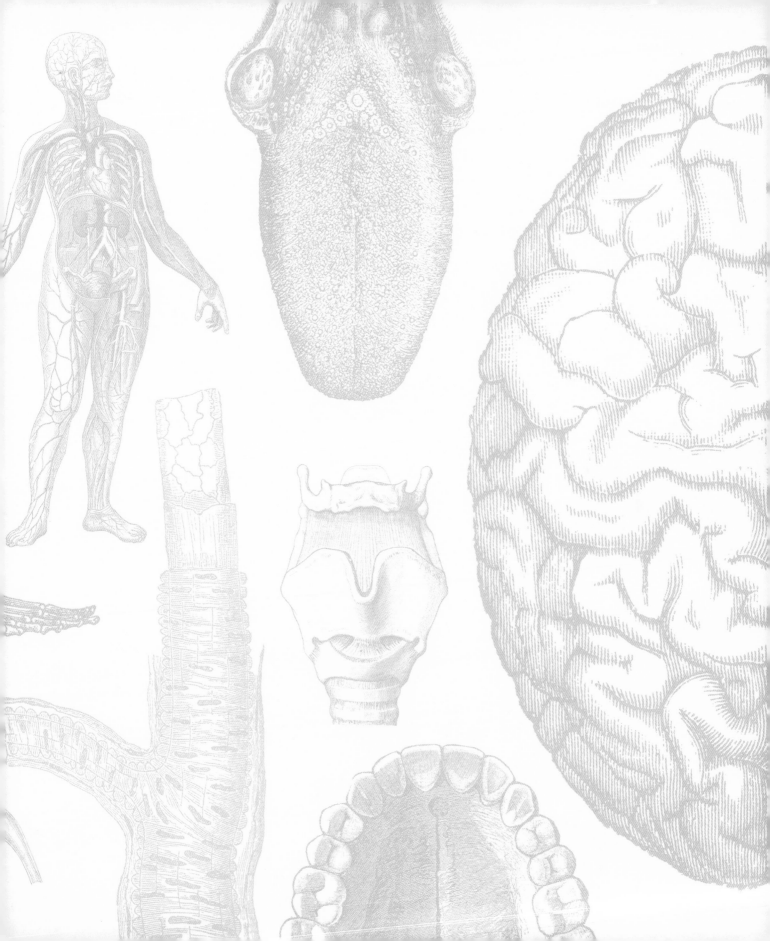

DR. FRANKENSTEIN'S
HUMAN BODY
BOOK

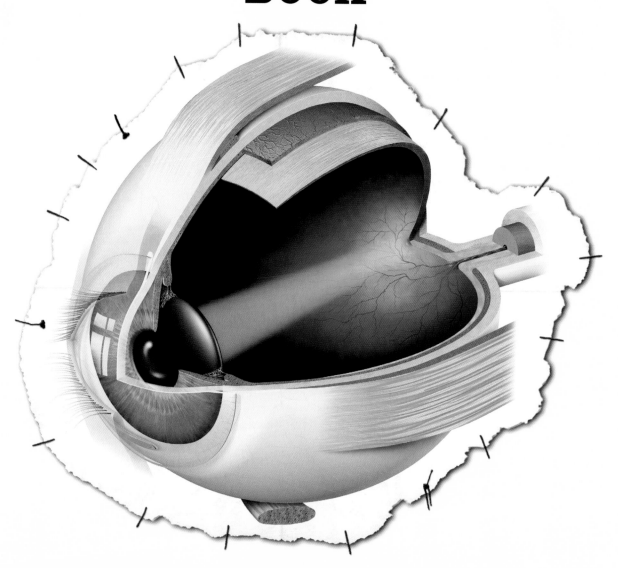

THE MONSTROUS TRUTH ABOUT HOW YOUR BODY WORKS

LONDON, NEW YORK, MELBOURNE,
MUNICH, AND DELHI

Author Richard Walker
Consultant Penny Preston
Artist Nick Abadzis

For Tall Tree Ltd.:
Editors Katie Dicker, Jon Richards
Designers Ed Simkins, Jonathan Vipond

For Dorling Kindersley:
Senior editor Andrea Mills
Senior art editor Philip Letsu
Managing editor Linda Esposito
Managing art editor Diane Thistlethwaite
Publishing manager Andrew Macintyre
Category publisher Laura Buller
Design development manager Sophia Tampakopoulos Turner
Production controller Angela Graef
Senior production editor Vivianne Ridgeway
Picture research Fran Vargo
Jacket editor Mariza O'Keeffe
Jacket designer Yumiko Tahata
US editor Margaret Parrish

This paperback edition published 2008
First published in the United States in 2008 by
DK Publishing 375 Hudson Street, New York, New York 10014

A catalog record for this book is available from the Library of Congress
ISBN: 978-0-7566-4281-5
Printed and bound by Leo Paper Products, China
Discover more at
www.dk.com

Contents

Dr. Frankenstein's masterplan

Come inside, Dr. Frankenstein's the name.
I'm sure you've heard it many times. Glad you could join me.
You find me in a state of excitement. In all my years
dedicated to the study of science and nature, this is the
most extraordinary experiment I've ever undertaken.

As you can see, my laboratory shelves are bursting with
body parts. Don't look so startled—that's everything we
need to make a living, breathing human being. As my
assistant, you'll be helping me every step of the way,
but be warned, this is not for the faint-hearted.

Now follow me. You are about to embark on
the experience of a lifetime...

Raw materials

First things first. Let's take a look at the raw materials needed to make a person. The simplest are incredibly tiny particles called atoms. They're used to make molecules that, in turn, build cells, the living units from which the body will be constructed.

light microscope

It would be impossible to see cells if it weren't for the microscope. A light microscope like this one can magnify a cell so you can see its basic features. But we need a more powerful instrument—an electron microscope—to reveal a cell's structure.

atoms and molecules

It takes trillions of atoms, arranged in a highly organized fashion, to make a body. Of the 20 different types of atom inside us, the top six are oxygen, carbon, hydrogen, nitrogen, calcium, and phosphorus. Atoms can exist on their own, but most prefer to link up and form molecules, such as water molecules, which can make up to 60 percent of a human's body weight.

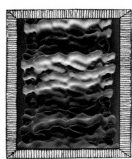

A cell membrane has two layers of molecules containing carbon, hydrogen, oxygen, nitrogen, and phosphorus atoms.

A water molecule is made of two hydrogen atoms (red) and one oxygen atom (yellow).

Cell membrane surrounds cell and controls what substances enter and leave it ___

Cytoplasm is a jellylike fluid in which organelles float

Day 1

This is history in the making. With the help of my new assistant, I can realize my dream—creating a human body. Assistant seems eager and enthusiastic. Has grasped the basics, assembled atoms, and surveyed cells. Now let's build some tissues.

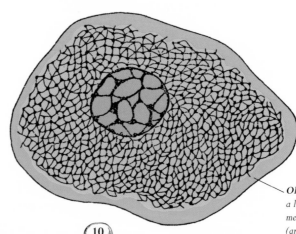

Old drawing of a cell, as seen with a light microscope, shows a thin cell membrane surrounding the cytoplasm (green and brown), and the nucleus (purple)

cells and organelles

Though tiny, cells are far from simple. Look carefully and you'll see that in between the cell membrane and the nucleus there are lots of tiny structures, called organelles. Each of these has its own job to do, but organelles also work together to bring the cell to life.

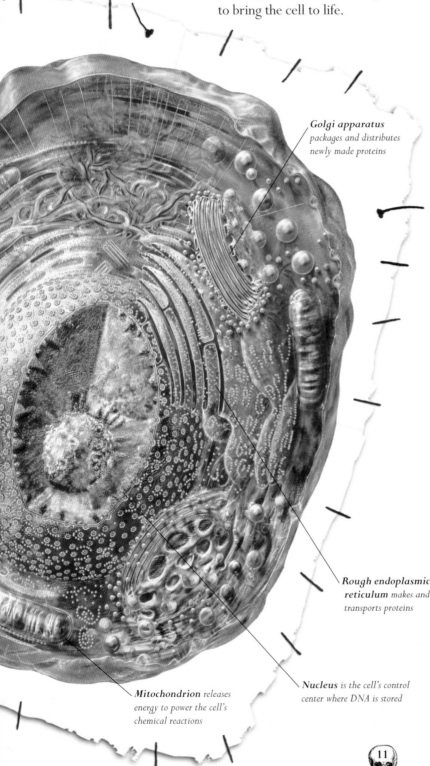

Golgi apparatus *packages and distributes newly made proteins*

Rough endoplasmic reticulum *makes and transports proteins*

Mitochondrion *releases energy to power the cell's chemical reactions*

Nucleus *is the cell's control center where DNA is stored*

⇒ DNA and proteins ⇐

Locked away inside the nucleus of every cell are 46 extremely long DNA molecules. These DNA molecules contain the 25,000 or so instructions we'll need to make a body. These instructions—called genes—control the production of proteins (substances that are, as we'll see, in charge of organizing all the body's other molecules).

DNA molecule *consists of two long, intertwined strands that coil up for easy storage*

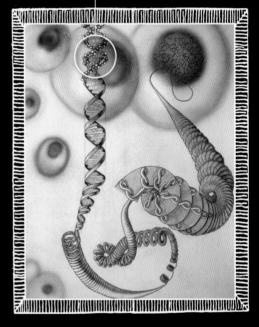

The most versatile of the body's molecules, proteins play key roles in building and running cells. The enzymes that control the chemical reactions of life are especially important. Proteins are formed from smaller molecules called amino acids.

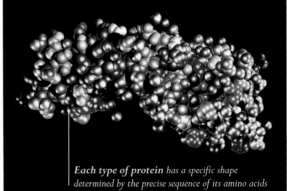

Each type of protein *has a specific shape determined by the precise sequence of its amino acids*

Tissues and organs

Building a body takes tens of trillions of cells. There are more than 200 different types of cell, each with its own shape, size, and job to do. Cells of the same or similar types organize themselves into groups called tissues. Two or more types of tissues form organs, such as the stomach.

organs and systems

The stomach is just one of the body's many organs. Other organs include the heart and the brain. A group of linked organs make up a system, such as the digestive system.

Stomach wall contains epithelial, connective, muscular, and nervous tissues

organ building

Cut a thin section through the folded wall of the stomach, put it under a microscope, and this is what you see. The white space is the inside of the stomach. A thin, dark pink layer of epithelial tissue covers a thicker, pale pink layer of connective tissue. Below that is some muscle tissue. Together these tissues contribute to building the stomach.

Connective tissue in the stomach wall holds other tissues together

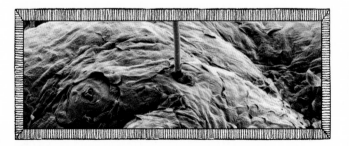

⟫ on the outside ⟪

Tissues aren't restricted to the inside of the body. This image (left), produced using a scanning electron microscope, shows the epidermis—a type of epithelial tissue—that forms the upper layer of the skin and covers the body.

line and cover

Epithelial tissue, or epithelium, is made from tightly packed cells. Epithelium lines and protects the insides (and covers the outsides) of organs that make up several body systems, such as the digestive, respiratory, and urinary systems. Touch the inside of your mouth and you are feeling epithelium. It also forms glands and the insides of blood vessels.

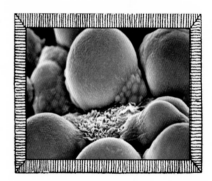

Epithelial cells *are closely packed in these ducts from the thyroid gland*

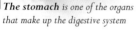

The stomach *is one of the organs that make up the digestive system*

support and package

Connective tissues include cartilage, bone, and other tissues that support the body and package its organs. They also include adipose tissue (right), which has plump fat-storing cells.

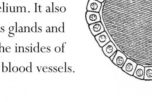

movement

Muscle tissue consists of cells that contract (get shorter) to produce movement. Skeletal muscle moves the body, smooth muscle (left) makes organs squeeze, and cardiac muscle makes the heart beat.

control

Nervous tissue is made from long, spiky cells that are linked into a massive network. They generate and carry electrical signals at high speed to control everything you do.

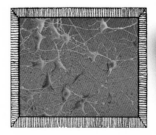

Day 2
Assistant is very organized—has made the connections and covered the topic with ease. Learned rapidly how to weave tissues into organs.

Bone basics

Time to get a grip! Grab hold of your wrist and squeeze gently. Does it collapse completely? No, because under your skin there are bones. Bones are produced from a mix of cells, mineral salts, and collagen fibers that makes them alive, hard, and strong, but not brittle. A combination of compact and spongy bone makes the skeleton as strong as steel, but a fraction of the weight.

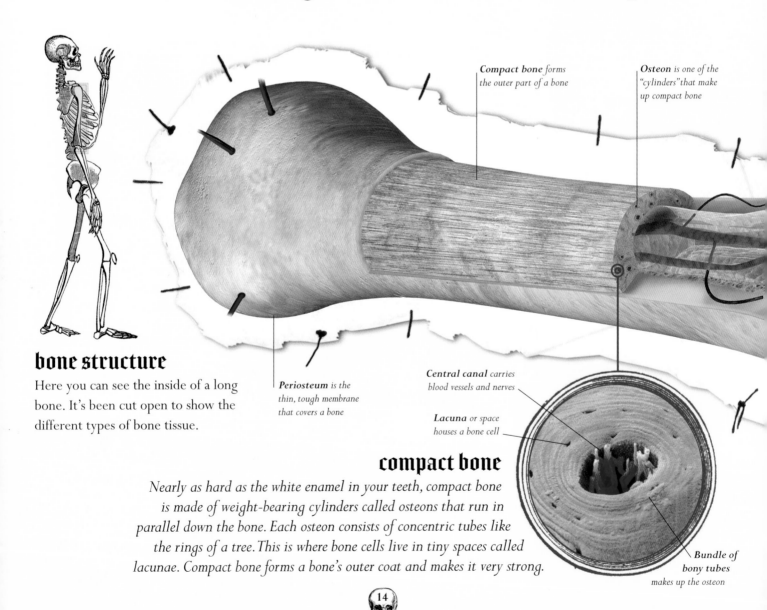

Compact bone forms the outer part of a bone

Osteon is one of the "cylinders" that make up compact bone

bone structure

Here you can see the inside of a long bone. It's been cut open to show the different types of bone tissue.

Periosteum is the thin, tough membrane that covers a bone

Central canal carries blood vessels and nerves

Lacuna or space houses a bone cell

compact bone

Nearly as hard as the white enamel in your teeth, compact bone is made of weight-bearing cylinders called osteons that run in parallel down the bone. Each osteon consists of concentric tubes like the rings of a tree. This is where bone cells live in tiny spaces called lacunae. Compact bone forms a bone's outer coat and makes it very strong.

Bundle of bony tubes makes up the osteon

spongy bone

If your bones were made solely from compact bone, they would be so heavy that you wouldn't be able to move. Fortunately, bones also contain lighter spongy bone consisting of strong, weight-bearing struts. In some bones, the spaces between the struts are filled with red bone marrow.

Spongy bone consists of a honeycomb of struts

Blood vessels supply bone cells with oxygen and food

Red blood cells newly formed in the red bone marrow

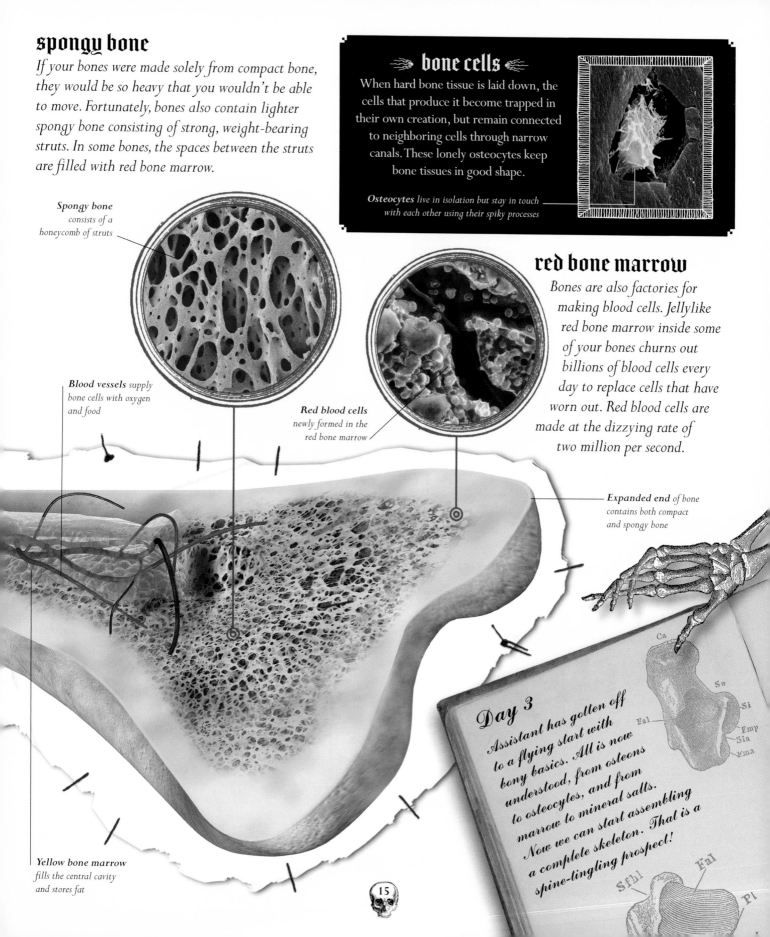

⇒ bone cells ⇐

When hard bone tissue is laid down, the cells that produce it become trapped in their own creation, but remain connected to neighboring cells through narrow canals. These lonely osteocytes keep bone tissues in good shape.

Osteocytes live in isolation but stay in touch with each other using their spiky processes

red bone marrow

Bones are also factories for making blood cells. Jellylike red bone marrow inside some of your bones churns out billions of blood cells every day to replace cells that have worn out. Red blood cells are made at the dizzying rate of two million per second.

Expanded end of bone contains both compact and spongy bone

Yellow bone marrow fills the central cavity and stores fat

Day 3

Assistant has gotten off to a flying start with bony basics. All is now understood, from osteons to osteocytes, and from marrow to mineral salts. Now we can start assembling a complete skeleton. That is a spine-tingling prospect!

Backbone and ribs

Whether you call it the backbone, vertebral column, or spine, this chain of bones forms the core of the skeleton. Everything else will hang from it. The S-shape of the upright spine gives it a natural springiness to absorb shocks during movement. With the backbone in place, the ribs can be added as well.

the spine

You'll see that the spine is built from a stack of 24 oddly shaped bones called vertebrae, along with a sacrum and coccyx. These four thoracic vertebrae show the basic structure of a vertebra, although they vary according to their type, position, and role.

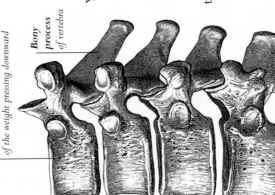

Bony *process* of vertebra

Body of vertebra carries most of the weight pressing downward

Facet forms joint with the end of a rib

Four thoracic vertebrae seen in side view

disks and movement

Each vertebra's chunky body is separated from that of its neighbor by a disk of cartilage with a squishy center. These disks protect the vertebrae from sudden shocks. They also allow bending and twisting movements that, when "added up" for the whole backbone, make it fairly flexible.

Intervertebral disks (green) are easy to see in this CT scan

Atlas and axis allow head to nod and shake

Joint between one vertebra and the next

Seven cervical vertebrae support the neck and head

Twelve thoracic vertebrae form joints with the ribs

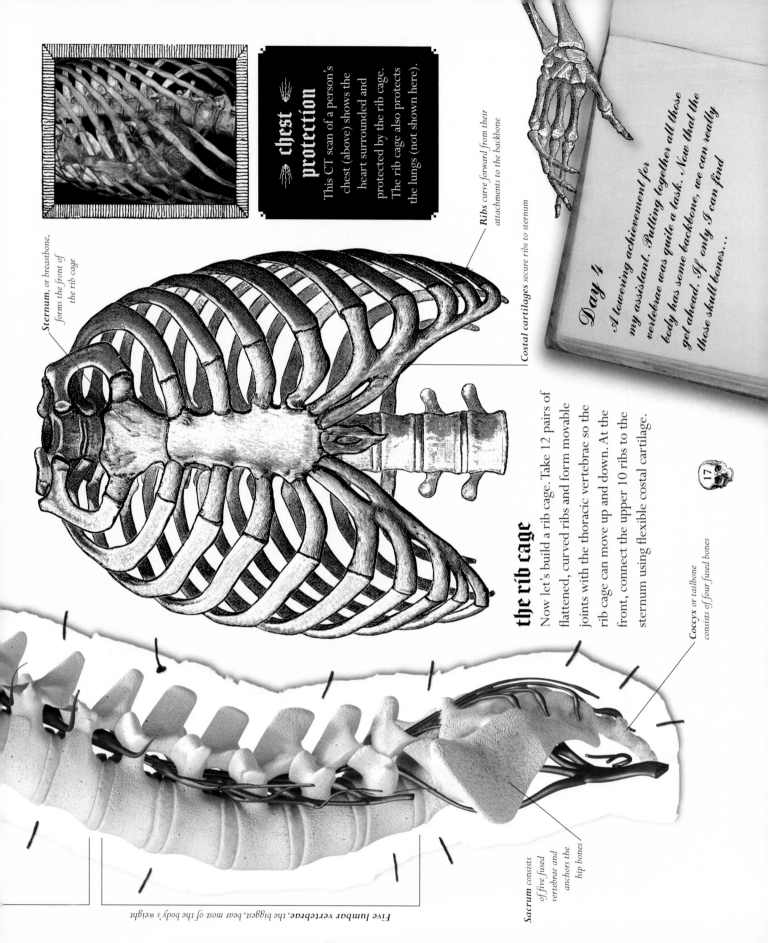

Sternum, or breastbone, forms the front of the rib cage

Ribs curve forward from their attachments to the backbone

Costal cartilages secure ribs to sternum

the rib cage

Now let's build a rib cage. Take 12 pairs of flattened, curved ribs and form movable joints with the thoracic vertebrae so the rib cage can move up and down. At the front, connect the upper 10 ribs to the sternum using flexible costal cartilage.

Coccyx or tailbone consists of four fused bones

Sacrum consists of five fused vertebrae and anchors the hip bones

Five lumbar vertebrae, the biggest, bear most of the body's weight

Day 4

A towering achievement for my assistant. Putting together all those vertebrae was quite a task. Now that the body has some backbone, we can really get ahead. If only I can find those skull bones...

17

Skull

Tap gently on the side of your head and what do you feel? Just under the skin is the most complex part of your skeleton—the skull. It's really important because it protects the brain, eyes, ears, tongue, and nose. The skull also helps to determine what the face looks like.

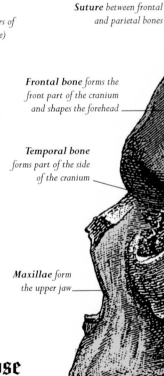

Skull X-ray *shows two pairs of sinuses (orange)*

losing weight

Some of the skull bones around the eye sockets contain hollow, air-filled spaces called sinuses. They make the skull a bit lighter in weight so it doesn't push down so much on the backbone. The sinuses are connected to the nose, so they also help moisten and warm breathed-in air.

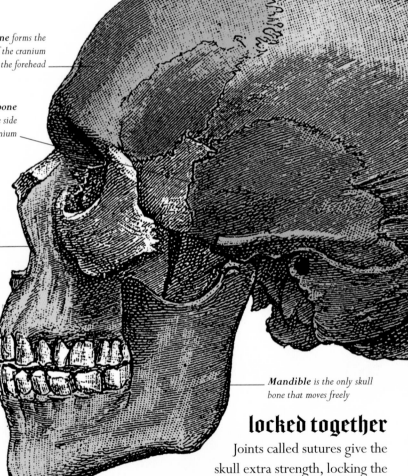

Suture *between frontal and parietal bones*

Frontal bone *forms the front part of the cranium and shapes the forehead*

Temporal bone *forms part of the side of the cranium*

Maxillae *form the upper jaw*

Mandible *is the only skull bone that moves freely*

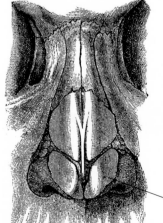

bendy nose

Bone isn't the only material used in the skeleton. Tough but flexible cartilage is found on bone ends, in ear flaps, and in the nose—give yours a tweak to feel it.

Alar cartilage *is one of several plates of cartilage that shape the nose*

locked together

Joints called sutures give the skull extra strength, locking the skull bones together like pieces in a jigsaw puzzle. Only the mandible moves to let you eat, drink, speak, and breathe.

bones of the skull

Here are the 28 bones—including six tiny ear bones—you'll need to construct a skull. The frontal, occipital, sphenoid, and ethmoid bones, plus the paired parietal and temporal bones, form the domed cranium around the brain. Fourteen bones form the framework of the face.

Parietal bones *form most of the top and sides of the cranium*

Occipital bone *forms most of the base of the cranium*

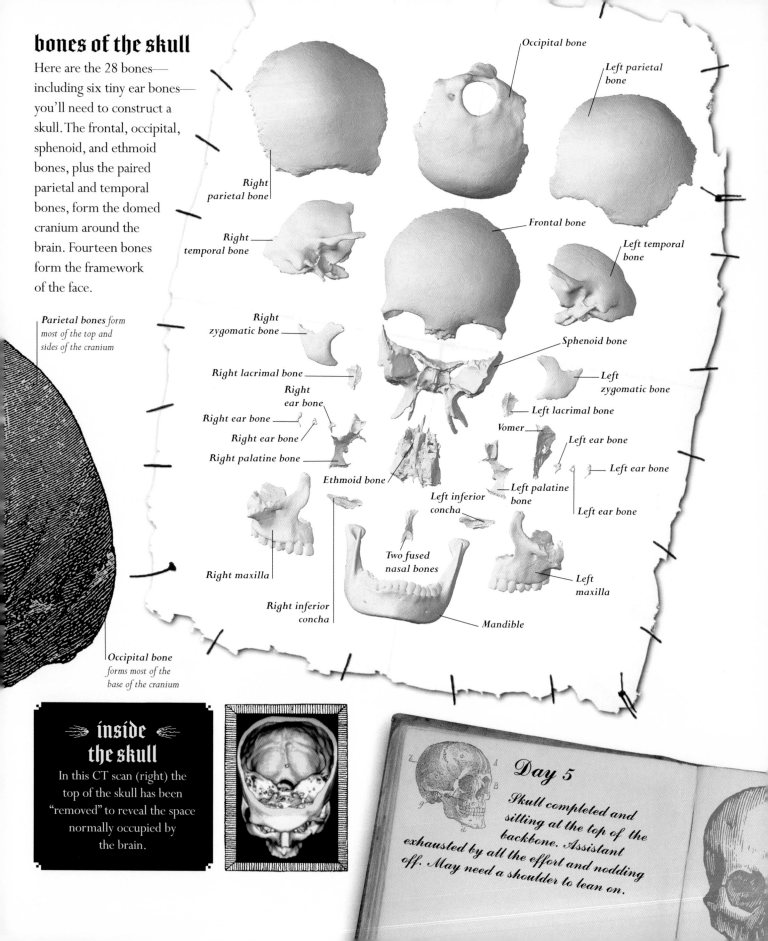

Occipital bone

Left parietal bone

Right parietal bone

Frontal bone

Right temporal bone

Left temporal bone

Right zygomatic bone

Sphenoid bone

Right lacrimal bone

Left zygomatic bone

Right ear bone

Left lacrimal bone

Right ear bone

Vomer

Right ear bone

Left ear bone

Right palatine bone

Left ear bone

Ethmoid bone

Left palatine bone

Left ear bone

Left inferior concha

Right maxilla

Two fused nasal bones

Left maxilla

Right inferior concha

Mandible

inside the skull

In this CT scan (right) the top of the skull has been "removed" to reveal the space normally occupied by the brain.

Day 5

Skull completed and sitting at the top of the backbone. Assistant exhausted by all the effort and nodding off. May need a shoulder to lean on.

Shoulders and arms

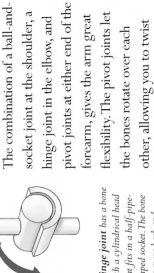

The time has come to add the highly versatile upper limbs to our growing skeleton. The shoulder blade fits onto the back of the rib cage, providing a handy joint to attach the upper arm bone (humerus). The humerus is linked to the two bones of the forearm (radius and ulna).

shoulder joint

This is the body's most freely moving joint. It's a ball-and-socket joint that allows movement in any direction. But that freedom comes at a price. The joint has to be held in place by all sorts of ligaments, muscles, and tendons.

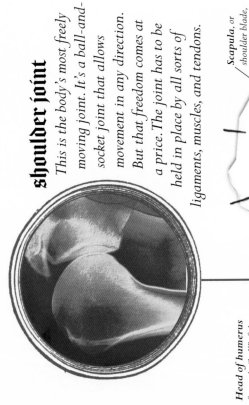

Head of humerus *forms the "ball" of the shoulder joint*

Scapula, *or shoulder blade, is flat and triangular*

Cavity in scapula *forms ball-and-socket joint with head of the humerus*

Humerus

flexible arms

The combination of a ball-and-socket joint at the shoulder, a hinge joint in the elbow, and pivot joints at either end of the forearm, gives the arm great flexibility. The pivot joints let the bones rotate over each other, allowing you to twist your hand.

Hinge joint *has a bone with a cylindrical head that fits in a half-pipe-shaped socket. The bone can move back and forward at one angle only.*

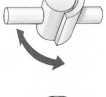

Ball-and-socket joint *contains a bone with a ball-shaped head that fits into a rounded socket. The ball is free to rotate in any direction.*

Rounded head *of humerus*

Shaft *of humerus*

End of humerus *forms part of elbow joint*

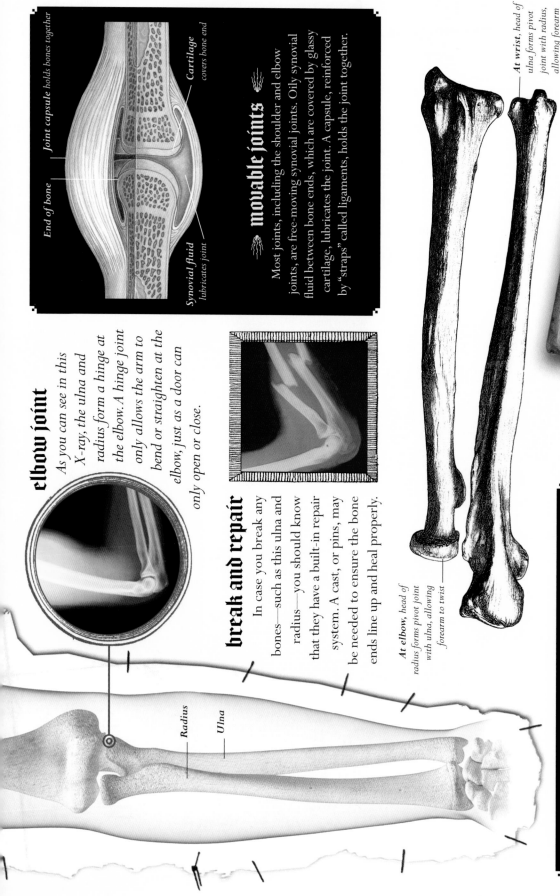

movable joints

Most joints, including the shoulder and elbow joints, are free-moving synovial joints. Oily synovial fluid between bone ends, which are covered by glassy cartilage, lubricates the joint. A capsule, reinforced by "straps" called ligaments, holds the joint together.

Joint capsule holds bones together

End of bone

Cartilage covers bone end

Synovial fluid lubricates joint

elbow joint

As you can see in this X-ray, the ulna and radius form a hinge at the elbow. A hinge joint only allows the arm to bend or straighten at the elbow, just as a door can only open or close.

break and repair

In case you break any bones—such as this ulna and radius—you should know that they have a built-in repair system. A cast, or pins, may be needed to ensure the bone ends line up and heal properly.

Radius

Ulna

At elbow, head of radius forms pivot joint with ulna, allowing forearm to twist

At wrist, head of ulna forms pivot joint with radius, allowing forearm to twist

reaching out

Arms are amazingly useful and practical. You can extend your arm in any direction in order to reach out to an object. This X-ray shows the bones and joints that provide this flexibility.

Day 6

Up to the elbows with work, assistant managed to put the humerus in the right place without hitting the funny bone. Understands now why joints don't creak when they move. But may need a hand with the next assignment.

21

Hands

The hands are made from lots of small bones with flexible joints. Hinged loosely at the end of the forearm, the hand can perform a range of movements. In particular, the thumb and fingers can grasp and manipulate objects. That's why the hands are so useful to my assistant!

Thumb, *or first digit, has only two phalanges*

Condyloid joint
between metacarpal and phalanx (finger bone)

flexible thumb

Of the five digits, the thumb is the most mobile. Thanks to a saddle joint at its base, where metacarpal meets carpal, the thumb can move across the palm of the hand and then turn inward to touch or oppose the tips of each of the fingers, as you can see in this X-ray.

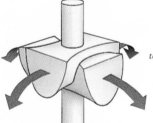

Carpal bones, together with the ends of the forearm bones, form the wrist

Plane joint
between carpal bones

A saddle joint *is very flexible, with bone ends that fit together like two saddles.*

A plane joint *forms where bone surfaces are nearly flat and allows only limited movement.*

Metacarpal bones *form the palm of the hand*

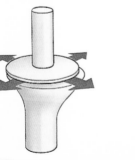

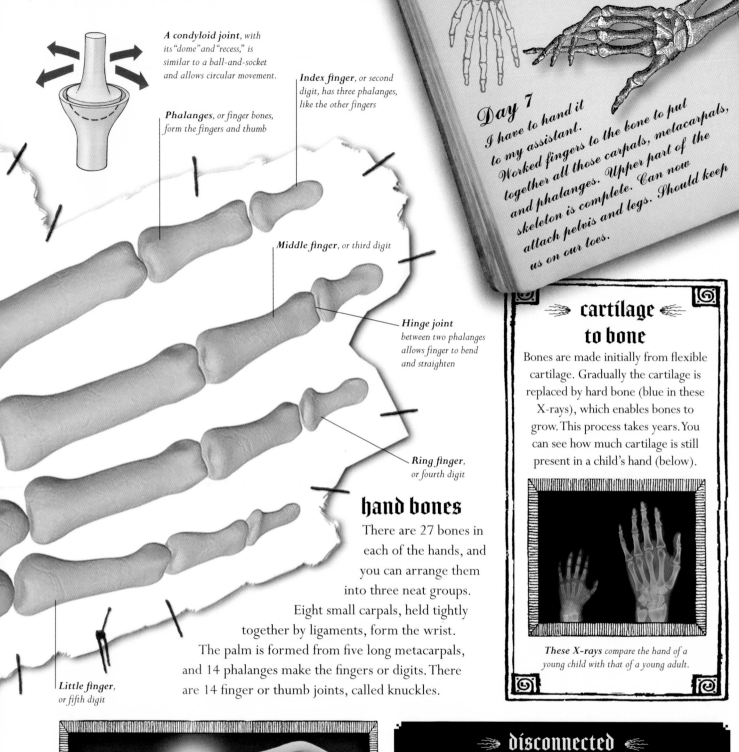

A condyloid joint, with its "dome" and "recess," is similar to a ball-and-socket and allows circular movement.

Phalanges, or finger bones, form the fingers and thumb

Index finger, or second digit, has three phalanges, like the other fingers

Middle finger, or third digit

Hinge joint between two phalanges allows finger to bend and straighten

Ring finger, or fourth digit

Little finger, or fifth digit

Day 7

I have to hand it to my assistant. Worked fingers to the bone to put together all those carpals, metacarpals, and phalanges. Upper part of the skeleton is complete. Can now attach pelvis and legs. Should keep us on our toes.

hand bones

There are 27 bones in each of the hands, and you can arrange them into three neat groups. Eight small carpals, held tightly together by ligaments, form the wrist. The palm is formed from five long metacarpals, and 14 phalanges make the fingers or digits. There are 14 finger or thumb joints, called knuckles.

cartilage to bone

Bones are made initially from flexible cartilage. Gradually the cartilage is replaced by hard bone (blue in these X-rays), which enables bones to grow. This process takes years. You can see how much cartilage is still present in a child's hand (below).

These X-rays compare the hand of a young child with that of a young adult.

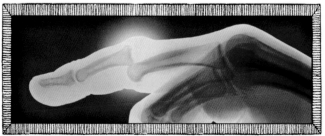

disconnected

A fall or other injury can force bones out of line so they become dislocated like these X-rayed finger bones (left). Surrounding nerves and ligaments may also be damaged. A doctor can manipulate the bones back to their correct positions.

Pelvis

Put your hands on your hips and you will feel your pelvis. This vital component anchors the legs to the backbone—so when you run in one direction, the rest of your body follows. The pelvis also supports the organs found in the abdomen, the area between the chest and the tops of the legs.

hip bones

When you were younger, each of your hip bones consisted of three separate bones called the ilium, ischium, and pubis. But as we get older, these bones fuse together into a single unit.

Illium is the largest of the three bones making a hip bone

leg link

The hip joint is formed where the "ball" of the thigh bone, or femur, meets the "socket" in the hip bone. This ball-and-socket joint is less flexible than the shoulder joint. The bones are held together by ligaments when you walk, run, or jump.

Ball-and-socket joint between hip bone and femur

Femur

Strong ligaments hold hip joint together and prevent bones separating

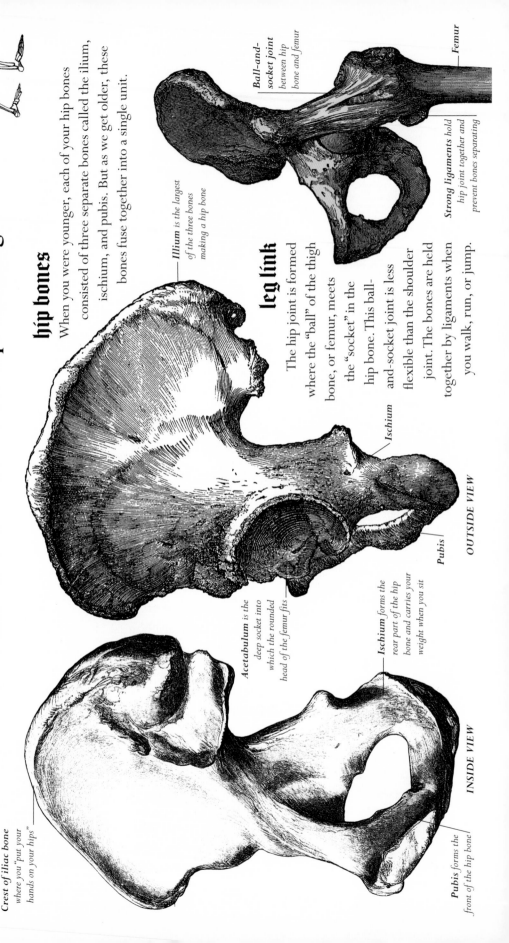

Ischium

OUTSIDE VIEW

Pubis

Acetabulum is the deep socket into which the rounded head of the femur fits

Ischium forms the rear part of the hip bone and carries your weight when you sit

Crest of iliac bone where you "put your hands on your hips"

Pubis forms the front of the hip bone

INSIDE VIEW

bony pelvis

Put the two hip bones together and you make the pelvic girdle. At the front, they meet at a slightly movable cartilage joint called the pubic symphysis. At the rear, they are anchored to the sacrum. The hip bones, sacrum, and coccyx form the bowl-shaped pelvis.

X-ray *showing the artificial components (pink) of a hip joint*

☞ artificial joint ☜

Joints damaged by injury or disease can be replaced. The ends of damaged bones are removed and replacement parts made of metal or plastic are inserted. A hip replacement is now a very common surgical procedure.

Sacrum, *part of the backbone, is attached to the two hip bones*

Ilium

Joint *between the sacrum and hip bone is stabilized by strong ligaments*

Pelvic inlet *is central space of pelvis*

Pubic symphysis *is where two hip bones are joined by a cartilage disk*

Pubis

Ischium

MALE PELVIS

male and female

It's time to check we're using the right pelvis for our creation. A man's pelvis is narrower and deeper than a woman's pelvis. A woman's pelvis has a wider pelvic inlet (opening). This allows space for a baby's head to go through when she gives birth.

FEMALE PELVIS

25

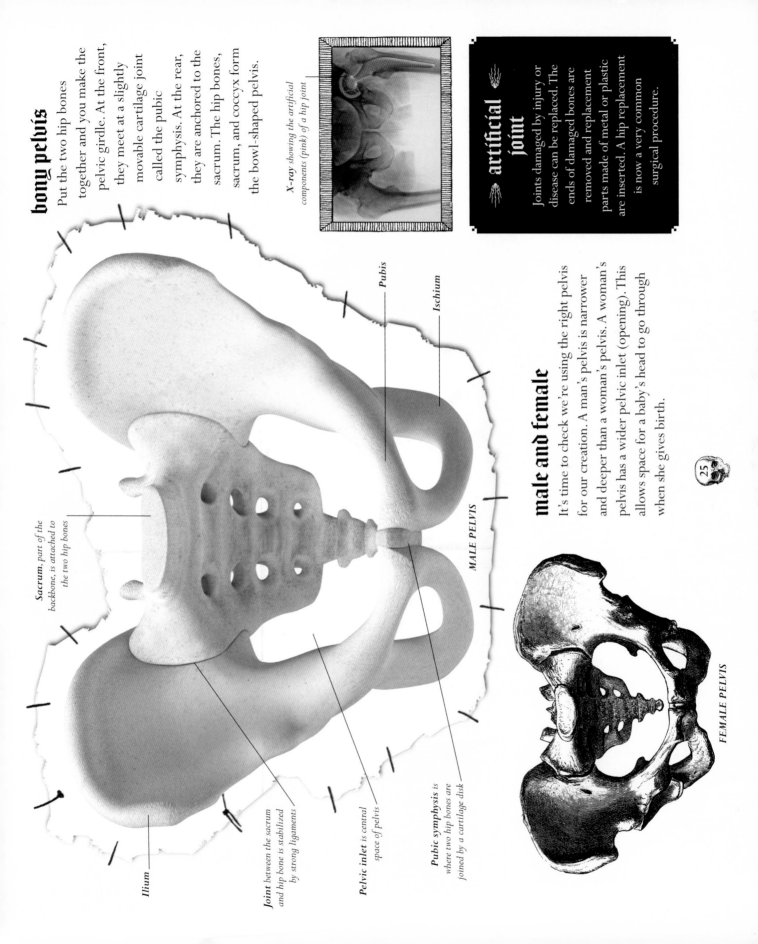

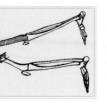

Legs and feet

Today's task is to assemble the bones of the legs and feet. They support the body and push it off the ground when you walk or run. One interesting design point: when the body is upright, the knees go into a "locked" position to save energy.

lower limbs

In terms of bones, the legs and feet bear a striking resemblance to the arms and hands.

However, the leg bones are carrying weight, so they are longer and stronger than those in the arms.

flexibility

Installing legs and feet is going to give our body a great variety of movement thanks to the combination of a ball-and-socket joint in the hip, and hinge joints at the knee and ankle.

Patella, or kneecap, protects the knee joint and aids the action of thigh muscles

knee joint

Located where the femur and tibia meet, the knee joint is a special kind of hinge joint that allows the leg to bend and straighten, but also rotate a little. Ligaments inside and outside the joint reinforce it. Cartilage inside the joint stabilizes it.

Knee joint is the biggest and most complex joint in the body

Head of femur *forms joint with hip bone*

Femur, *or thigh bone, is the body's longest and strongest bone*

the foot

Each foot is made from 26 bones organized as seven tarsals, five metatarsals, and 14 phalanges. The arrangement is similar to the hands, but the feet are less flexible because the toes are short, and strong ligaments bind the bones together. The foot forms a strong base for standing and running. This platform is also curved, giving added springiness during movement.

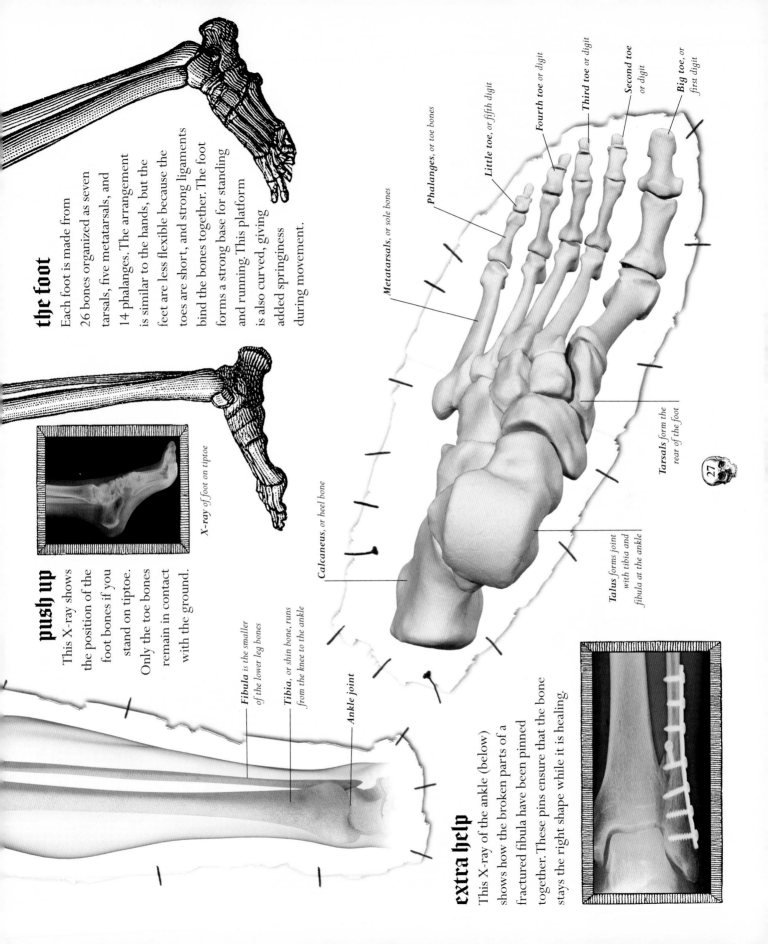

X-ray of foot on tiptoe

push up

This X-ray shows the position of the foot bones if you stand on tiptoe. Only the toe bones remain in contact with the ground.

Fibula *is the smaller of the lower leg bones*

Tibia, *or shin bone, runs from the knee to the ankle*

Ankle joint

Calcaneus, *or heel bone*

Metatarsals, *or sole bones*

Phalanges, *or toe bones*

Little toe, *or fifth digit*

Fourth toe *or digit*

Third toe *or digit*

Second toe *or digit*

Big toe, *or first digit*

Tarsals *form the rear of the foot*

Talus *forms joint with tibia and fibula at the ankle*

extra help

This X-ray of the ankle (below) shows how the broken parts of a fractured fibula have been pinned together. These pins ensure that the bone stays the right shape while it is healing.

Skeleton

Thanks to some sterling work, we have now put the 206 bones in place, together with joints and ligaments, to make an entire skeleton. With this movable scaffolding in position, anything is possible. We could add muscles to move those bones—but that's for the future. You should now check that your knowledge of the skeleton is complete.

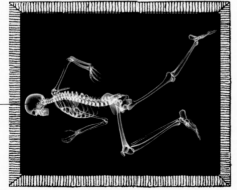

A skeleton in motion shows how flexible it is

support and movement

Here's your checklist of what the skeleton does for the body. It provides support, protects internal organs, and allows the body to move in lots of different ways.

A radionuclide, or gamma scan, of the skeleton from the back.

bone scan

This is a different way of looking at bones. An injected radioactive chemical is taken up by bone cells and reveals, in a scan, which parts of the skeleton are more active (red) or less active (blue).

two in one

A skeleton has two main sections. The axial part forms the core, or axis, of the skeleton. The appendicular part attaches the limbs to the axis.

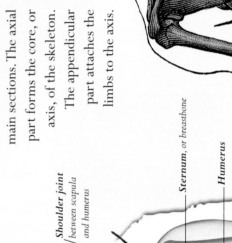

Axial skeleton (yellow) consists of skull, sternum, ribs, and backbone

Backbone, or vertebral column

Scapula, or shoulder blade, seen more clearly in rear view

Skull houses brain and sense organs

Shoulder joint between scapula and humerus

Sternum, or breastbone

Humerus

Clavicle, or collarbone, forms pectoral girdle with scapula

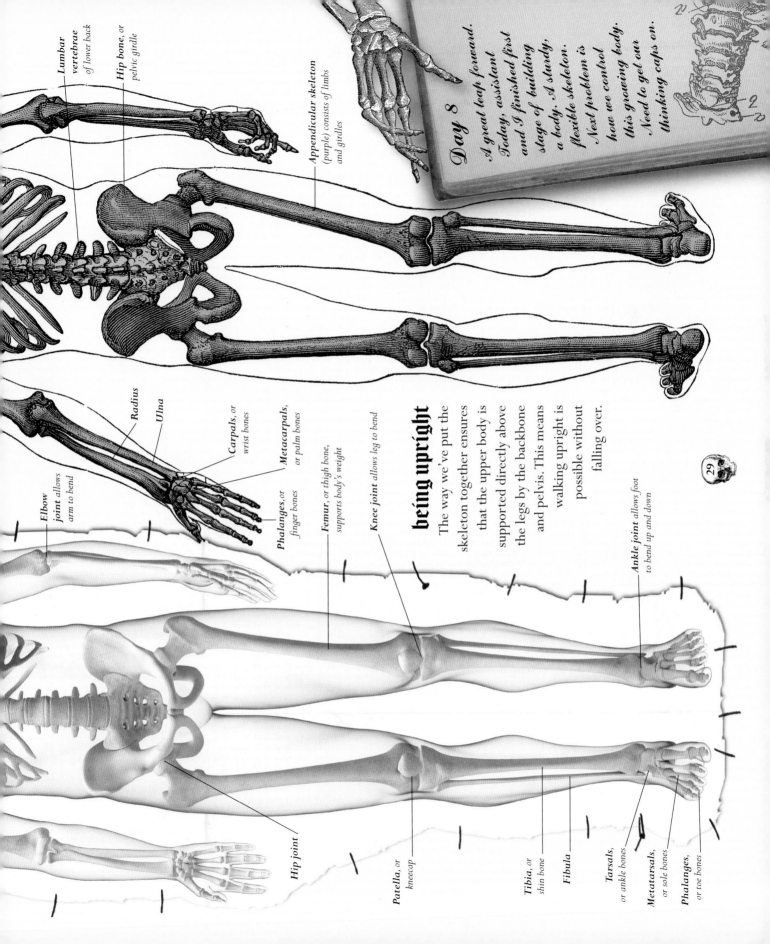

Lumbar vertebrae of lower back

Hip bone, or pelvic girdle

Appendicular skeleton (purple) consists of limbs and girdles

Radius

Ulna

Carpals, or wrist bones

Metacarpals, or palm bones

Phalanges, or finger bones

Elbow joint allows arm to bend

Femur, or thigh bone, supports body's weight

Knee joint allows leg to bend

being upright

The way we've put the skeleton together ensures that the upper body is supported directly above the legs by the pelvis. This means walking upright is possible without falling over.

Ankle joint allows foot to bend up and down

Hip joint

Patella, or kneecap

Tibia, or shin bone

Fibula

Tarsals, or ankle bones

Metatarsals, or sole bones

Phalanges, or toe bones

Day 8

A great leap forward.
Today, assistant
and I finished first
and I finished first
stage of building
a body. A sturdy,
flexible skeleton.
Next problem is
how we control
this growing body.
Need to get our
thinking caps on.

Cerebrum

Working as my assistant involves a great deal of observation, learning, remembering, and imagining. All those facilities are provided by the cerebrum, the key part of the brain. Its thin outer layer, the cortex, enables you to see, feel, think about, and respond to the world around you.

control center

Making up about 85 percent of the brain, the cerebrum is undoubtedly the brain's control center. It is divided into two halves, or hemispheres, each responsible for the opposite half of the body.

Premotor cortex *controls complex movements such as riding a bike*

Prefrontal cortex *is involved in thought, planning, and personality*

Deep groove *divides cerebrum into left and right hemispheres*

Right hemisphere *controls left-hand side of body and deals with art and music*

Broca's area *controls speech*

Left hemisphere *controls right-hand side of body and deals with language and math*

brain cells

You had better start counting because there are about 100 billion neurons, or nerve cells, in the cerebrum. Each one receives electrical signals from, and sends them to, thousands of other neurons through processes called dendrites and axons.

working areas

The cerebral cortex has certain areas that perform specific tasks: sensory areas receive messages from sensors in the skin and other places; motor areas send out instructions to muscles to move the body; and association areas analyze and interpret information.

Motor cortex *triggers muscles into movement*

Primary sensory cortex *enables you to feel touch and pain*

Sensory association cortex *interprets signals from skin receptors*

Wernicke's area *interprets the words you hear and see*

Visual association cortex *analyzes patterns of visual information to form images*

Primary visual cortex *interprets signals from the eyes about shapes, colors, and movement*

Primary auditory cortex *receives signals from the ears*

Auditory association cortex *analyzes and identifies sounds and their sources*

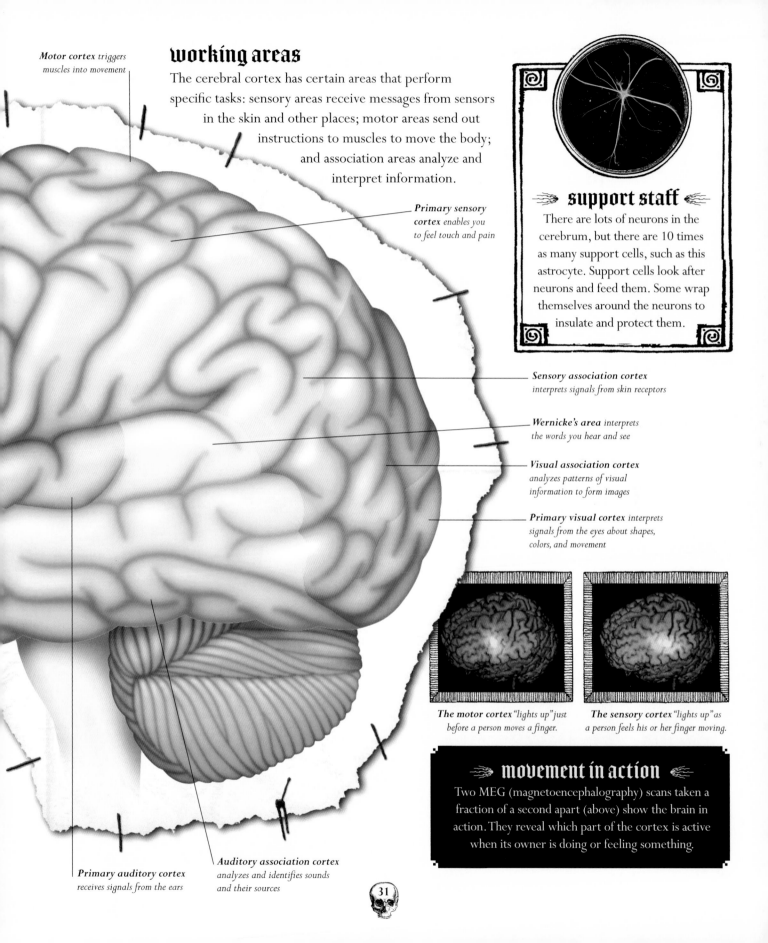

support staff

There are lots of neurons in the cerebrum, but there are 10 times as many support cells, such as this astrocyte. Support cells look after neurons and feed them. Some wrap themselves around the neurons to insulate and protect them.

The motor cortex *"lights up" just before a person moves a finger.*

The sensory cortex *"lights up" as a person feels his or her finger moving.*

movement in action

Two MEG (magnetoencephalography) scans taken a fraction of a second apart (above) show the brain in action. They reveal which part of the cortex is active when its owner is doing or feeling something.

Central nervous system

Brain is at the core of the central nervous system

Once installed, the brain needs to be linked up to the rest of the body. The first part of that process is to add the spinal cord. Together, the brain and spinal cord form the central nervous system, a command center that receives, analyzes, and stores incoming information and sends out instructions.

Left and right hemispheres separated to show "inner brain"

Inner view of left hemisphere of cerebrum

BACK

in control

The central nervous system controls and coordinates most of what is going on inside the body, including the way you are turning the pages as you read this book.

Spinal cord relays messages to and from the brain

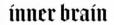

Cerebellum controls balance and helps coordinate movement

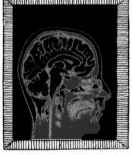

inner brain

The cerebrum dominates the brain landscape, so you need to get inside it to see what else is happening. If you slice through the corpus callosum—the mass of axon connections that links the two halves of the cerebral cortex—the hemispheres come apart.

Brain stem connects brain to spinal cord and automatically controls heart rate and breathing

Spinal cord

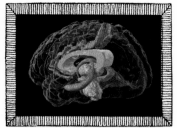

Spinal cord seen in rear view

spinal cord

Starting at the base of the brain and running down most of the length of the backbone, the spinal cord relays information to and from the brain. But it also processes information. It controls many automatic reactions, called reflexes, such as automatically pulling your hand away from a hot object to keep from getting burned.

Corpus callosum is a band of axons that connects the left and right hemispheres

surround and protect

With the consistency of warm jelly, the brain can easily be damaged. It floats in a fluid, which cushions it from sudden jolts, and is surrounded by three layers of protective membranes and the skull (right).

Thalamus relays and filters messages going to cerebral cortex

Hypothalamus regulates many body activities including hunger, thirst, and sleep, and controls the pituitary gland

FRONT

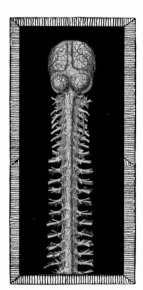

Brain and spinal cord showing short spinal nerves.

Pituitary gland controls other hormone-releasing glands

protective tunnel

The spinal cord runs down the back along a "tunnel" created by the bony arches of neighboring vertebrae in the backbone. This tunnel protects the spinal cord and its billions of neurons from damage.

Day 9
Today, assistant and I used our gray matter to install a brain that thinks, feels, and tells its owner what to do. Added a spinal cord down the back. It's time to wire them up to the rest of the body.

Nerves

The next task is to hook up the brain and the spinal cord to the rest of the body, so the central nervous system can do its job. That's achieved through a massive network of cables, called nerves, that carry high-speed electrical signals to and from every nook and cranny of the body.

communication cables

Nerves are organized bundles of the long axons of neurons (nerve cells) that carry electrical signals to and from the central nervous system. There are 12 pairs of cranial nerves coming from the brain and brain stem, and 31 pairs of spinal nerves sprouting from the spinal cord.

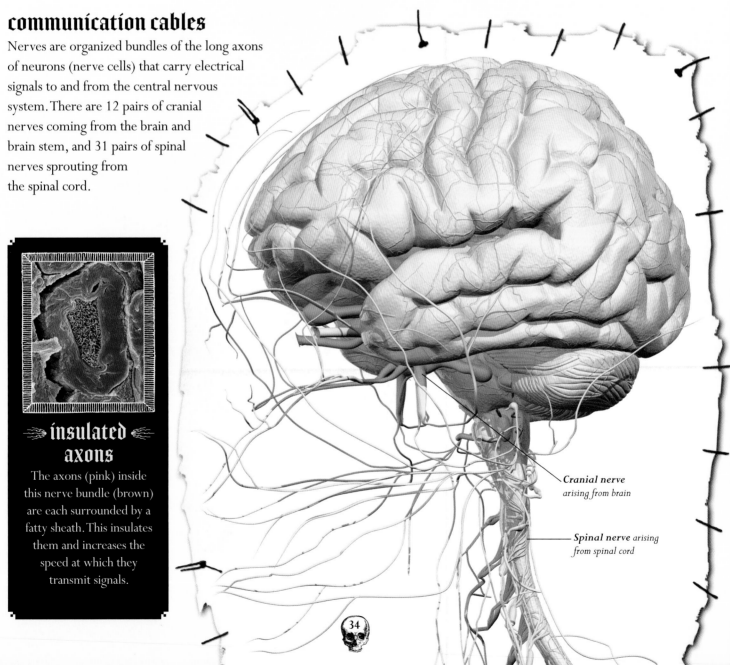

insulated axons

The axons (pink) inside this nerve bundle (brown) are each surrounded by a fatty sheath. This insulates them and increases the speed at which they transmit signals.

Cranial nerve arising from brain

Spinal nerve arising from spinal cord

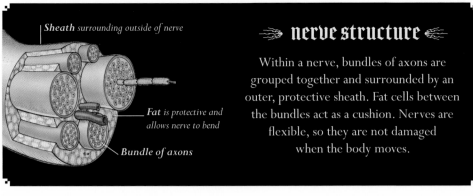

Sheath *surrounding outside of nerve*

Fat *is protective and allows nerve to bend*

Bundle of axons

nerve structure

Within a nerve, bundles of axons are grouped together and surrounded by an outer, protective sheath. Fat cells between the bundles act as a cushion. Nerves are flexible, so they are not damaged when the body moves.

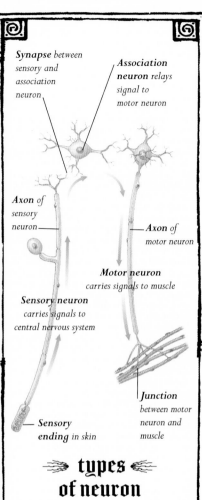

Synapse *between sensory and association neuron*

Association neuron *relays signal to motor neuron*

Axon *of sensory neuron*

Axon *of motor neuron*

Motor neuron *carries signals to muscle*

Sensory neuron *carries signals to central nervous system*

Junction *between motor neuron and muscle*

Sensory ending *in skin*

types of neuron

There are three types of neuron. Sensory neurons are triggered by physical stimuli, and carry signals from sensors to the central nervous system. Motor neurons carry instructions to muscles. Association neurons in the central nervous system relay signals between sensory and motor neurons, and process information.

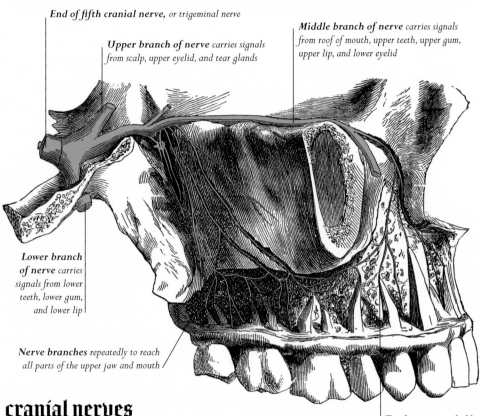

End of fifth cranial nerve, *or trigeminal nerve*

Upper branch of nerve *carries signals from scalp, upper eyelid, and tear glands*

Middle branch of nerve *carries signals from roof of mouth, upper teeth, upper gum, upper lip, and lower eyelid*

Lower branch of nerve *carries signals from lower teeth, lower gum, and lower lip*

Nerve branches *repeatedly to reach all parts of the upper jaw and mouth*

Tooth nerve *numbed by dentists to prevent pain*

cranial nerves

Most cranial nerves supply the head and neck. Here you can see some of the branches of one of those nerves as it reaches out to parts of the face, mouth, and teeth. Ouch!

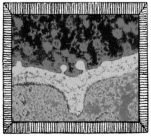

synapse

A synapse is a junction between the ends of neurons where they are very close but do not touch. The neurons communicate with one another by sending chemical messengers across this synaptic gap.

Gap (yellow) between ends of two neurons (blue and green)

Day 10
No longer feeling nervous. Everything is under control and the system is buzzing with electricity. Assistant about to research vision. Hope we see eye to eye over this.

Eyes

The eyes are the body's most important sense organs. Whatever the conditions, automatic mechanisms ensure that the eye receives the right amount of light and focuses a sharp image on its light receptors. These send signals to the brain that enable you to see what is in front of you.

Day 11

Assistant has seen the light. Now understands eye focus and can tell rods from cones. An excellent pupil. Next job—to keep an eye out for some ears.

changing shape

The lens changes shape to form a sharp image on the retina whether we look at near or distant objects. A ring of ciliary muscle (yellow/orange) around the lens controls changes in lens shape.

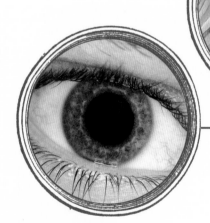

pupil control

Each pupil is a hole in the center of the colored iris through which light enters the back of the eye. By making the pupil smaller, the iris ensures that you're not dazzled by bright light. By making it bigger, the eye receives more light in darker conditions.

Pupil

Iris *controls size of pupil*

Eyelashes *protect eyes from dust and excess light*

Lens *alters shape to focus light on the retina*

Cornea *helps to focus light entering eye*

Conjunctiva *is a thin, moist, protective membrane*

optic nerves

Signals from each eye travel toward the brain along an optic nerve. The two nerves partly cross over, so that signals from the right halves of both eyes go to the right side of the brain, and vice versa.

Section through left eyeball, *seen from above*

Right eyeball

Muscle *that moves eyeball*

Right optic nerve

Cross-over of optic nerves

Dark choroid layer *contains blood vessels that supply retina and sclera*

Retina *is thin layer packed with light detectors*

Vitreous humor *is jellylike fluid that shapes the eye*

Optic nerve *carries signals to the brain*

light receptors

There are two types of light receptor. Six million cones work best in bright light and provide color vision, while 120 million rods work in dim light and produce black-and-white images.

Cone

Rod

One of six muscles *that move eyeball*

Sclera *is tough, white outer coat of eyeball*

seeing things

You don't actually see with your eyes. Their light receptors send signals to the back region of each hemisphere of the cerebrum. Here, they are interpreted and rebuilt into images that you see and recognize.

MRI *scan shows "slice" through head, revealing eyes and brain.*

Ears

Listen carefully, because it's time to assemble the ears. Most of the ear is protected inside the temporal bone of the skull. It's here that sound waves traveling through the air are detected.

inside the ear

Look inside the ear and you'll discover three zones. The outer part is the ear canal. The air-filled middle section has the eardrum at one end and the oval window at the other. The fluid-filled inner section has the cochlea and balance sensors.

outer canal

Sounds are created when objects vibrate and produce pressure waves in the air. These sound waves enter the ear canal. Earwax (right) is produced to clean the canal and to deter insects.

ossicles

The three ear bones, or ossicles, are the smallest bones in the body. The tiniest, the stirrup, is no bigger than a grain of rice. The others are called the hammer and the anvil.

transmit and amplify

The ossicles transmit vibrations from the eardrum to the oval window. When the eardrum vibrates, the bones move the oval window, sending vibrations through fluid in the inner ear. This action also amplifies the sound.

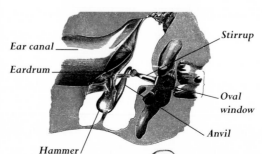

Ear canal

Eardrum

Stirrup

Oval window

Anvil

Hammer

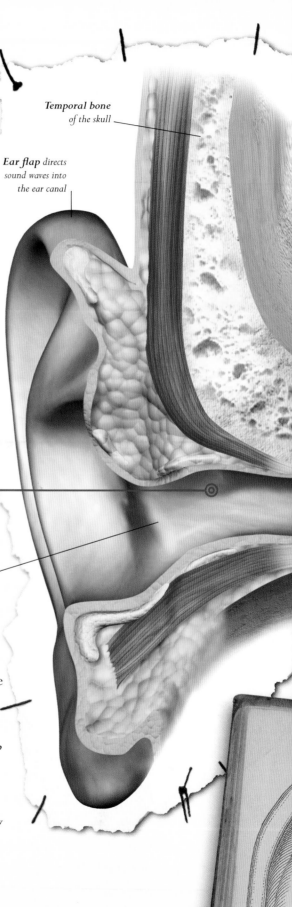

Temporal bone *of the skull*

Ear flap *directs sound waves into the ear canal*

Ear canal *carries sound into the ear*

ear drum

When sound waves hit the eardrum (left, red) it vibrates. These vibrations are passed to the ossicles. The hammer (orange) is attached to the eardrum.

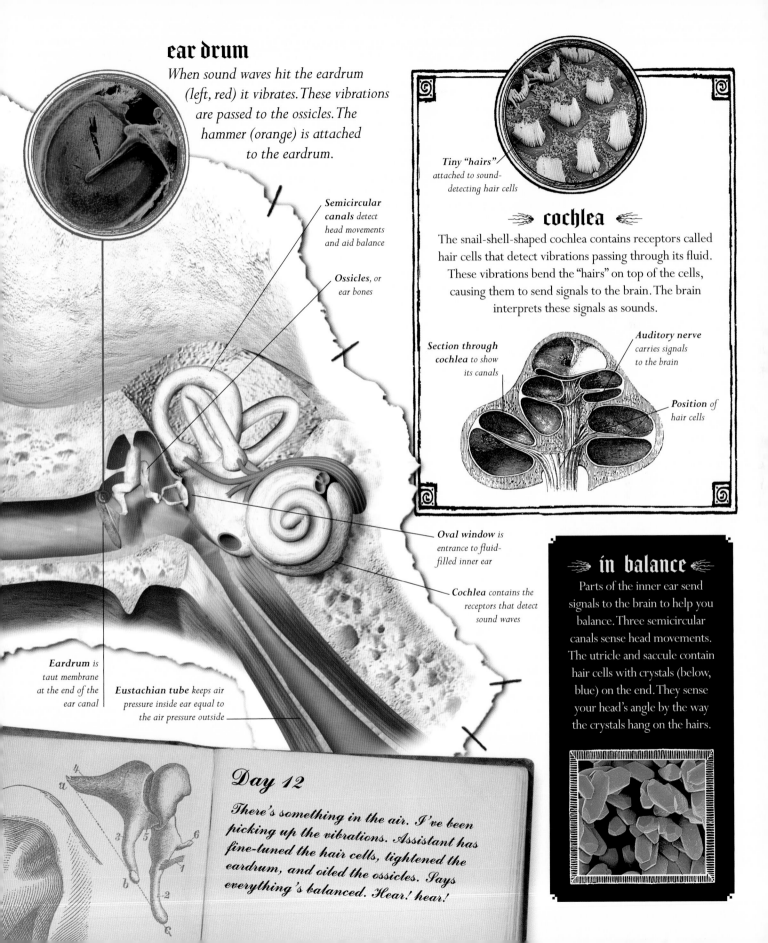

Tiny "hairs" attached to sound-detecting hair cells

cochlea

The snail-shell-shaped cochlea contains receptors called hair cells that detect vibrations passing through its fluid. These vibrations bend the "hairs" on top of the cells, causing them to send signals to the brain. The brain interprets these signals as sounds.

Section through cochlea to show its canals

Auditory nerve carries signals to the brain

Position of hair cells

Semicircular canals detect head movements and aid balance

Ossicles, or ear bones

Oval window is entrance to fluid-filled inner ear

Cochlea contains the receptors that detect sound waves

Eardrum is taut membrane at the end of the ear canal

Eustachian tube keeps air pressure inside ear equal to the air pressure outside

in balance

Parts of the inner ear send signals to the brain to help you balance. Three semicircular canals sense head movements. The utricle and saccule contain hair cells with crystals (below, blue) on the end. They sense your head's angle by the way the crystals hang on the hairs.

Day 12

There's something in the air. I've been picking up the vibrations. Assistant has fine-tuned the hair cells, tightened the eardrum, and oiled the ossicles. Says everything's balanced. Hear! hear!

Control systems

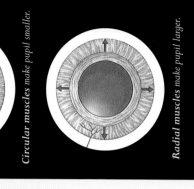

Circular muscles make pupil smaller.

Radial muscles make pupil larger.

autonomic nervous system

You probably didn't know about this "hidden" branch of the nervous system, but you'd be lost without it. It carries instructions to internal organs and regulates what they do. For example, it controls the muscles that make the pupil wider or narrower.

Without some form of control, body processes would go their own way at their own pace. There would be chaos. Fortunately, the two control systems we've installed keep things in order. The nervous system uses high-speed electrical signals for immediate effect. The endocrine system releases chemicals that work more slowly.

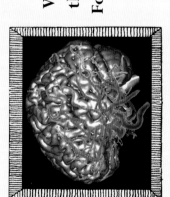

busy brain

This special X-ray (above) shows the mass of blood vessels that supply the brain with blood. They are needed because the busy brain consumes one-fifth of the body's oxygen and glucose, even though it makes up just 2 percent of the body's weight.

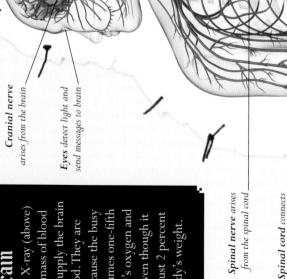

Cerebrum is the largest and most complex part of the brain

Cerebellum makes sure we move smoothly and stay upright

Cranial nerve arises from the brain

Eyes detect light and send messages to brain

Spinal nerve arises from the spinal cord

Spinal cord connects brain to spinal nerves

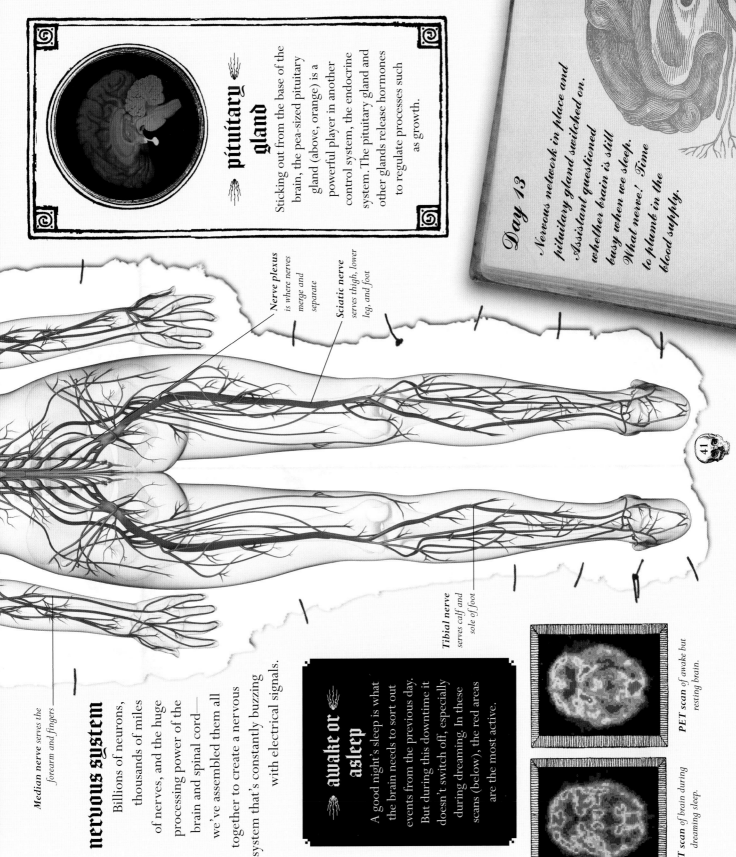

pituitary gland

Sticking out from the base of the brain, the pea-sized pituitary gland (above, orange) is a powerful player in another control system, the endocrine system. The pituitary gland and other glands release hormones to regulate processes such as growth.

Day 13

Nervous network in place and pituitary gland switched on. Assistant questioned whether brain is still busy when we sleep. What nerve! Time to plumb in the blood supply.

Median nerve serves the forearm and fingers

Nerve plexus is where nerves merge and separate

Sciatic nerve serves thigh, lower leg, and foot

Tibial nerve serves calf and sole of foot

nervous system

Billions of neurons, thousands of miles of nerves, and the huge processing power of the brain and spinal cord—we've assembled them all together to create a nervous system that's constantly buzzing with electrical signals.

awake or asleep

A good night's sleep is what the brain needs to sort out events from the previous day. But during this downtime it doesn't switch off, especially during dreaming. In these scans (below), the red areas are the most active.

PET scan of awake but resting brain.

PET scan of brain during dreaming sleep.

41

Blood vessels

Now that the bones are in place, we need to lay down the body's supply system. This consists of a vast network of blood vessels called arteries, veins, and capillaries that, stretched out, would wrap around the Earth four times. Blood vessels carry blood that delivers essential supplies to the body's cells.

living tubes

Blood vessels are "living tubes" because they are made from living cells. They vary in size from the biggest arteries and veins, which are the width of your thumb, to tiny capillaries, which you'll need a microscope to see. Let's compare arteries and veins.

Basilic vein carries blood from the hand and arm

arteries

Carrying oxygen-rich blood from the heart to the tissues, arteries have thick walls with layers of muscular and elastic tissues. The walls expand and recoil— you can feel this as a "pulse"— every time blood is pumped through them by the heart.

Brachial artery supplies blood to the upper arm

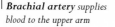

ARTERY

VEIN

veins

These vessels carry oxygen-poor blood from the tissues to the heart. The blood is under much lower pressure than in the arteries, which is why veins have relatively thin walls and a bigger central space. Veins have valves to stop blood from flowing "backward."

Thick muscle and elastic layers in the wall of the artery

viewing vessels

This image (left) shows blood vessels inside the chest of a person. It's produced using a technique called MRA (magnetic resonance angiography). The big arching vessel in the middle is the aorta, the artery that carries oxygen-rich blood from the heart.

Radial artery supplies blood to the wrist, thumb, and index finger

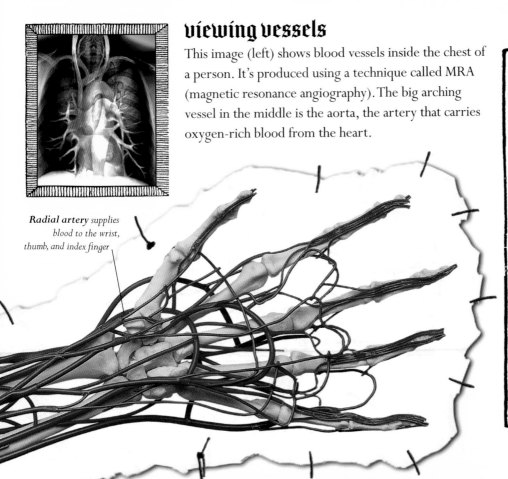

❧ cell supplies ❧

This is a unique view of the capillary network. As cells are never far from one of these tiny capillaries, there's no danger of them going short of essential supplies, such as food and oxygen, or being unable to get rid of unwanted waste.

❧ capillary link ❧

Capillaries may be microscopic, but they make up an amazing 98 percent of the total length of the blood vessel network. They arise from the narrowest artery branches, and carry blood through the tissues before merging to form the smallest vein branches. That means they link arteries to veins. That's some feat of plumbing!

Arteriole is the smallest branch of an artery

Venule is the smallest branch of a vein

Vein

Capillary network between cells

Artery

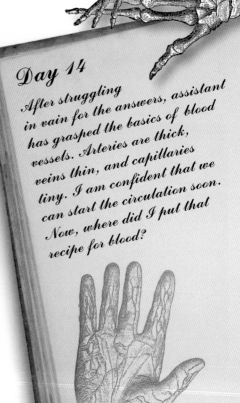

Day 14

After struggling in vain for the answers, assistant has grasped the basics of blood vessels. Arteries are thick, veins thin, and capillaries tiny. I am confident that we can start the circulation soon. Now, where did I put that recipe for blood?

Blood

Now the blood vessels are in place, they can be filled. Ten pints (five liters) of blood flow around the body, delivering oxygen, food, and other essentials to cells, as well as removing waste material. Blood also fights infection by destroying disease-causing microorganisms called pathogens.

hemoglobin

Blood cells are red because they're packed with an orange-red-colored protein called hemoglobin. Each molecule of this special substance can pick up four oxygen molecules in the lungs and deliver them to the body's cells. With 250 million hemoglobin molecules inside one red blood cell, that's one billion oxygen molecules carried per cell. And with 25 trillion red blood cells traveling around your body, that's... well, you do the math.

Hemoglobin *molecule consists of four iron-containing subunits*

Lymphocytes *release pathogen-disabling proteins called antibodies*

Red blood cell's *dimpled disk shape provides large surface for picking up oxygen*

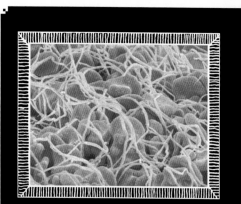

A net of fibrin threads traps red and other blood cells to make a blood clot.

⇒ repair kit ⇐

If a blood vessel is damaged, by a cut in the skin, for example, a self-repair mechanism automatically halts blood loss. First, platelets stick to each other in order to temporarily plug the leak. Then they trigger the conversion of a dissolved blood protein into fibers that create a blood clot to seal the wound.

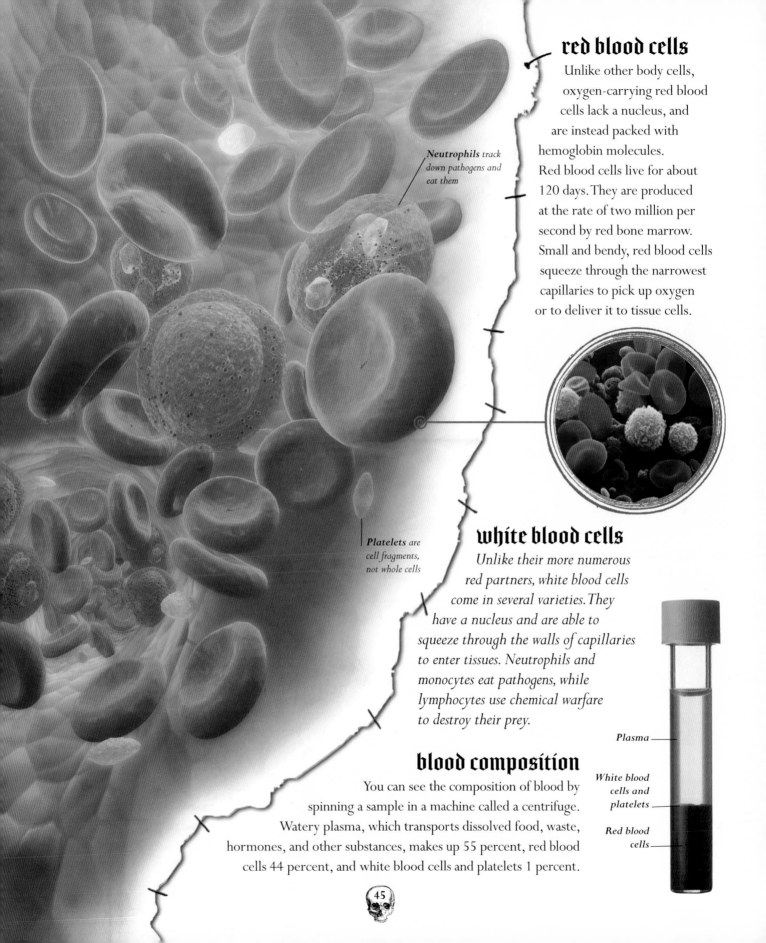

red blood cells

Unlike other body cells, oxygen-carrying red blood cells lack a nucleus, and are instead packed with hemoglobin molecules. Red blood cells live for about 120 days. They are produced at the rate of two million per second by red bone marrow. Small and bendy, red blood cells squeeze through the narrowest capillaries to pick up oxygen or to deliver it to tissue cells.

Neutrophils track down pathogens and eat them

Platelets are cell fragments, not whole cells

white blood cells

Unlike their more numerous red partners, white blood cells come in several varieties. They have a nucleus and are able to squeeze through the walls of capillaries to enter tissues. Neutrophils and monocytes eat pathogens, while lymphocytes use chemical warfare to destroy their prey.

blood composition

You can see the composition of blood by spinning a sample in a machine called a centrifuge. Watery plasma, which transports dissolved food, waste, hormones, and other substances, makes up 55 percent, red blood cells 44 percent, and white blood cells and platelets 1 percent.

Plasma

White blood cells and platelets

Red blood cells

Heart

Let's get to the heart of the matter. Working tirelessly to push blood around the body, the heart has separated left and right sides, each with two chambers. Both sides contract together about once a second, the right side pumping blood to the lungs, the left pumping blood to the body.

Superior vena cava *carries oxygen-poor blood from the upper body to the right atrium*

coronary supply

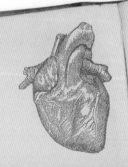

The blood rushing through the heart cannot supply the heart's muscle cells with fuel and oxygen. A separate blood supply is provided by the coronary arteries that arise from the aorta and branch throughout the heart wall.

one way

Two sets of valves guarantee a one-way flow of blood through the heart. Without these valves, blood would flow in two directions and would not circulate around the body. Each valve has flaps that open to allow blood through, and close to stop it from flowing backward.

Right atrium *receives oxygen-poor blood from the body and houses the heart's "pacemaker"*

heartstrings

Known as heartstrings, these tough cords connect the flaps of the bicuspid and tricuspid valves to the ventricle walls. When the ventricles contract, the heartstrings stop the valves from turning inside out like an umbrella in a gale.

Inferior vena cava *carries oxygen-poor blood from the lower body to the right atrium*

semilunar valves

Each semilunar valve has three pocketlike flaps that flatten as blood rushes between them during contraction. They fill up and block the exit to prevent blood from flowing backward during relaxation.

Day 15

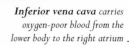

Today we are halfway through the project. Assistant has never lost heart, nor missed a pulse, and works as hard as cardiac muscle. Now's our chance to arm the defense force.

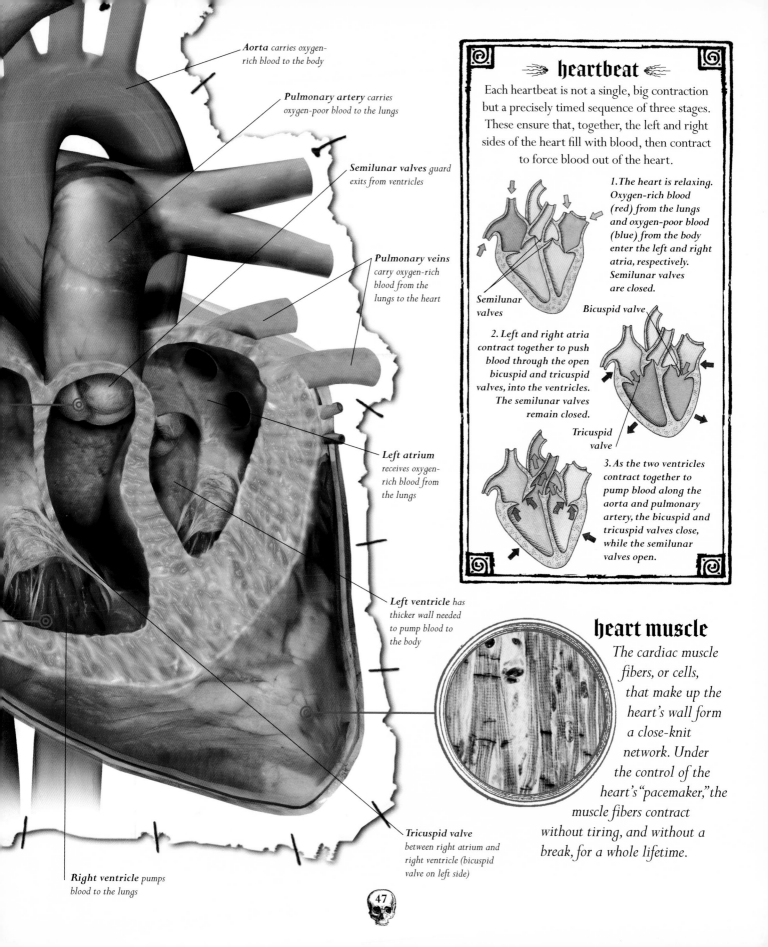

Aorta carries oxygen-rich blood to the body

Pulmonary artery carries oxygen-poor blood to the lungs

Semilunar valves guard exits from ventricles

Pulmonary veins carry oxygen-rich blood from the lungs to the heart

Left atrium receives oxygen-rich blood from the lungs

Left ventricle has thicker wall needed to pump blood to the body

Tricuspid valve between right atrium and right ventricle (bicuspid valve on left side)

Right ventricle pumps blood to the lungs

☞ heartbeat ☜

Each heartbeat is not a single, big contraction but a precisely timed sequence of three stages. These ensure that, together, the left and right sides of the heart fill with blood, then contract to force blood out of the heart.

1. The heart is relaxing. Oxygen-rich blood (red) from the lungs and oxygen-poor blood (blue) from the body enter the left and right atria, respectively. Semilunar valves are closed.

Semilunar valves

Bicuspid valve

2. Left and right atria contract together to push blood through the open bicuspid and tricuspid valves, into the ventricles. The semilunar valves remain closed.

Tricuspid valve

3. As the two ventricles contract together to pump blood along the aorta and pulmonary artery, the bicuspid and tricuspid valves close, while the semilunar valves open.

heart muscle

The cardiac muscle fibers, or cells, that make up the heart's wall form a close-knit network. Under the control of the heart's "pacemaker," the muscle fibers contract without tiring, and without a break, for a whole lifetime.

Lymph vessels and nodes

As the circulatory system performs its delivery service to cells, it leaves behind fluid in the tissues. We need to install a system of tubes to drain excess fluid, now called lymph, and return it to the blood. On the way, defense cells will destroy disease-causing pathogens in the lymph.

lymph nodes

Like beads on a string, these bean-shaped swellings occur along lymph vessels. Lymph nodes contain immune system cells—macrophages, which trap and engulf debris and bacteria, and lymphocytes, which disable or destroy specific enemies.

Lymph node *processes lymph flowing through it*

Thoracic duct *is a major lymphatic vessel*

one-way vessels

Lymph vessels are blind-ending and carry lymph in one direction. They have no "pump" to push lymph through them. Instead they're squeezed by skeletal muscles and equipped with valves to prevent backflow.

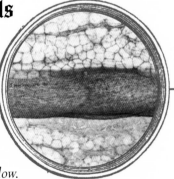

chemical warfare

Two groups of lymphocytes—B cells and T cells—are the lynchpins of the immune system. Each type of cell works in a different way, but both attack specific pathogens and retain a "memory" of them should they return to attack the body again.

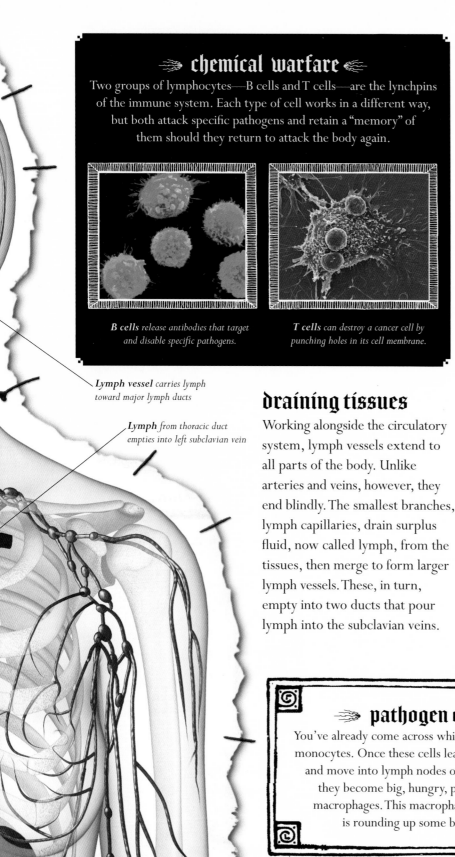

B cells *release antibodies that target and disable specific pathogens.*

T cells *can destroy a cancer cell by punching holes in its cell membrane.*

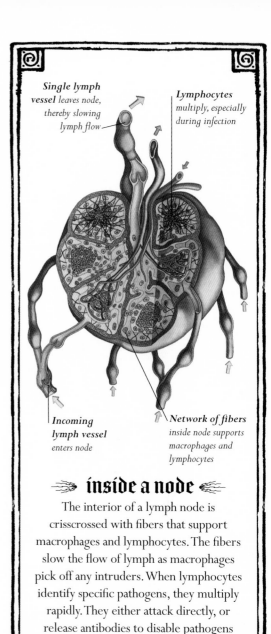

Single lymph vessel *leaves node, thereby slowing lymph flow*

Lymphocytes *multiply, especially during infection*

Incoming lymph vessel *enters node*

Network of fibers *inside node supports macrophages and lymphocytes*

Lymph vessel *carries lymph toward major lymph ducts*

Lymph *from thoracic duct empties into left subclavian vein*

draining tissues

Working alongside the circulatory system, lymph vessels extend to all parts of the body. Unlike arteries and veins, however, they end blindly. The smallest branches, lymph capillaries, drain surplus fluid, now called lymph, from the tissues, then merge to form larger lymph vessels. These, in turn, empty into two ducts that pour lymph into the subclavian veins.

inside a node

The interior of a lymph node is crisscrossed with fibers that support macrophages and lymphocytes. The fibers slow the flow of lymph as macrophages pick off any intruders. When lymphocytes identify specific pathogens, they multiply rapidly. They either attack directly, or release antibodies to disable pathogens for macrophages to attack.

pathogen eaters

You've already come across white blood cells called monocytes. Once these cells leave the bloodstream and move into lymph nodes or infected tissues, they become big, hungry, pathogen-eating macrophages. This macrophage (right, gold) is rounding up some bacteria (red).

Transportation systems

Once the body is complete, its trillions of cells will demand first-class transportation systems. The circulatory system delivers essential materials to every cell and removes waste products. The lymphatic system drains excess fluid from the tissues and helps the circulatory system to defend the body against pathogens.

taken to the top

This MRA image (below) shows the left and right common carotid arteries that carry blood up the neck to the head. At the bottom, you can see the curving aortic arch from which the arteries arise.

Common carotid artery *carries blood to head and brain*

Internal jugular vein *carries blood from the brain*

Aortic arch

Aorta *carries blood away from heart*

Double circulation

Time for you to discover how blood is pumped along to linked "loops" centered on the heart. One loop carries blood to the lungs to pick up oxygen. The other loop carries blood to the body's tissues to give up oxygen.

Pulmonary circulation *carries blood between heart and lungs*

Systemic circulation *carries blood between heart and the rest of the body*

Heart *is the circulatory system's pump*

Inferior vena cava *carries blood to heart*

circulatory system

Put together the heart, blood vessels, and blood and you get the circulatory or cardiovascular system. You can see the major veins in blue and the major arteries in red. The exceptions are the pulmonary artery (which carries oxygen-poor blood) and the pulmonary vein (which carries oxygen-rich blood).

changing color

Although we've color-coded blood vessels red or blue to show whether or not they are carrying oxygen-rich blood, they aren't really that color, nor is the blood inside them. But blood does change color as it travels around the body. Oxygen-rich blood is bright red (far right), while oxygen-poor blood is a darker purple-red.

Day 16

Transportation systems have proved tricky. Assistant did something wrong and it made my blood boil. Never mind, the job's done now, and the assistant is ready for a course in waste disposal.

Femoral vein *carries blood from the thigh*

Femoral artery *supplies the thigh and knee*

Lymph vessels *drain excess fluid from the tissues*

Anterior tibial artery *supplies the leg and foot*

lymphatic system

This network of blind-ending tubes is the body's second, and less famous, transportation system. As you will have seen already, its tiny capillaries scoop up excess fluid from the body's tissues, then its lymph vessels carry that fluid—called lymph—to be returned to the bloodstream. As this is going on, lymph flows through lymph nodes that filter out debris and pathogens.

Kidneys

It's important that the composition of blood circulating around the body is kept constant so cells live in stable conditions. We need to add two blood-filtering kidneys at the back of the abdomen. The kidneys remove poisonous waste and excess water, which they combine to make urine. This is later released from the body through the ureter.

filtration units

Each of the million nephrons in a kidney consists of a cluster of capillaries, called a glomerulus (below, pink), and a coiled tubule. Liquid filtered from the glomerulus is processed as it passes along the tubule, returning "useful" substances to the blood and leaving urine to flow into the pelvis.

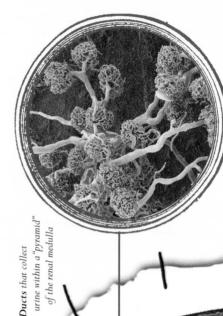

Renal capsule *is a protective layer that surrounds the kidney*

Renal medulla *is the zone within the renal cortex*

Ducts *that collect urine within a "pyramid" of the renal medulla*

adrenal gland

An adrenal gland, which sits on top of each kidney, releases several hormones, including adrenaline, into the bloodstream. The adrenaline-releasing cells (blue, shown above) surround a vein. If the body is under threat, adrenaline works with the nervous system to help combat stress.

Renal pelvis *is hollow funnel that directs urine into the ureter*

Renal artery *carries blood into the kidney*

The two kidneys (shown in the angiogram, below) receive one-quarter of the heart's output of blood. That's the daily equivalent of 12 bathtubs full of blood, from which just ½ gallon (1.5 liters) of urine is produced.

urine producer

Look inside a kidney and its structure is clear to see. There is a cortex surrounding the "pyramids" of the medulla that lead to the hollow pelvis. Nephrons in the outer cortex and medulla filter blood to make urine. This flows down collecting ducts to the pelvis, and on to the ureter.

Day 17

Assistant making frequent trips to the bathroom. Must be drinking too much water. But helps in understanding how kidneys filter blood to make urine. Now the kidneys are in place!

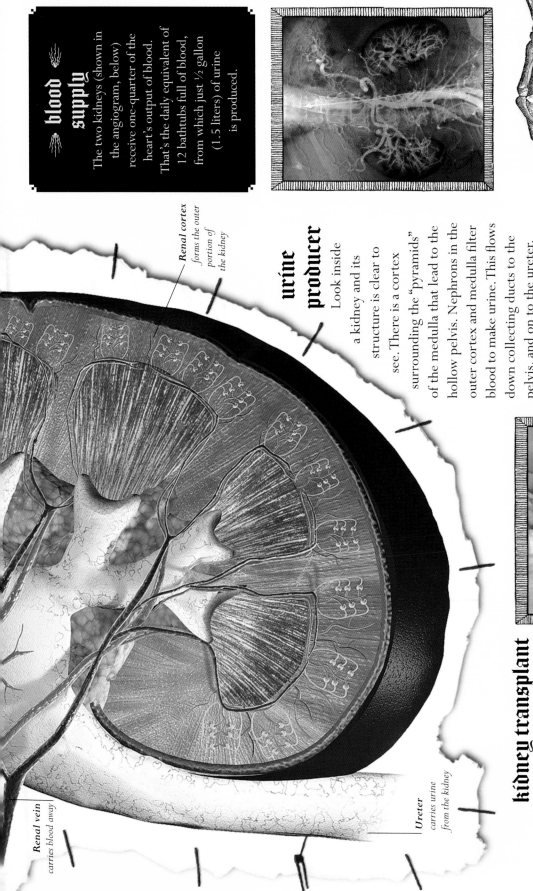

Renal cortex *forms the outer portion of the kidney*

Renal vein *carries blood away*

Ureter *carries urine from the kidney*

kidney transplant

This is a living kidney, taken from one person (the donor) and about to be moved or transplanted into the body of another person (the recipient) who needs it. The donated kidney will take over the functions of the recipient's kidneys, which have stopped working due to damage or disease.

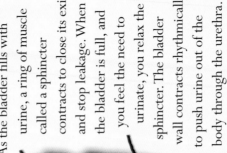

Urinary system

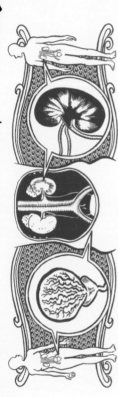

Working day and night, your kidneys release a constant trickle of urine. Without some means of storing urine, life would be very unpleasant. That's why we've added other parts of the urinary system. Urine is delivered by two ureters to a very stretchy, muscular bag called the bladder. This stores urine until you feel the need to release it through the urethra.

store and release

As the bladder fills with urine, a ring of muscle called a sphincter contracts to close its exit and stop leakage. When the bladder is full, and you feel the need to urinate, you relax the sphincter. The bladder wall contracts rhythmically to push urine out of the body through the urethra.

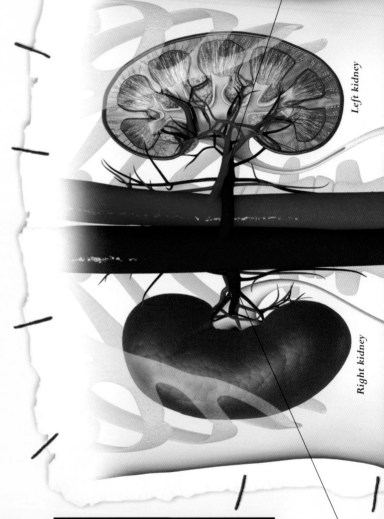

Renal artery branches from aorta and carries blood to kidney

Left kidney

Right kidney

Renal vein carries blood away from kidney

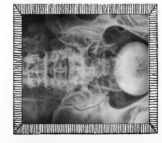

Filling

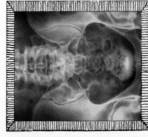

Emptying

fill and empty

You can see in these special X-rays a bladder (above, green) filling and emptying. As the bladder fills, receptors in its stretched wall send messages to your brain, so you feel the urge to urinate.

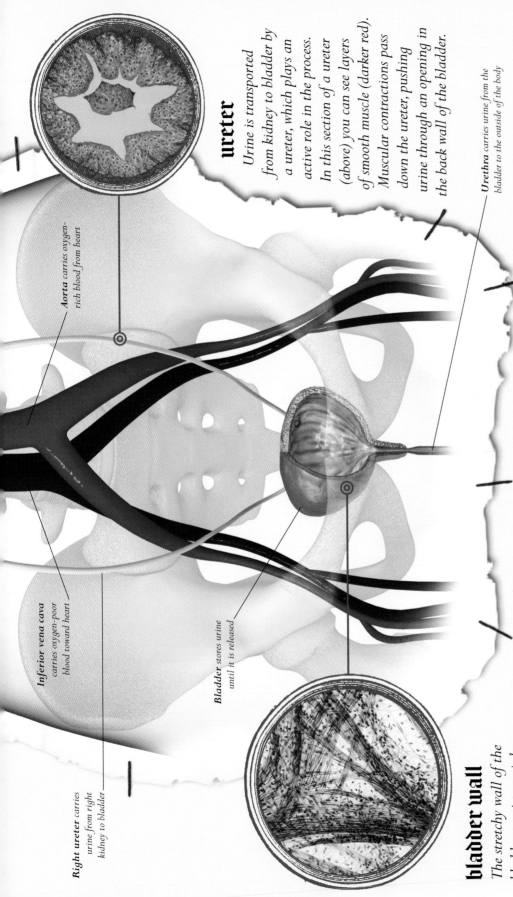

ureter

Urine is transported from kidney to bladder by a ureter, which plays an active role in the process. In this section of a ureter (above) you can see layers of smooth muscle (darker red). Muscular contractions pass down the ureter, pushing urine through an opening in the back wall of the bladder.

Aorta *carries oxygen-rich blood from heart*

Urethra *carries urine from the bladder to the outside of the body*

Inferior vena cava *carries oxygen-poor blood toward heart*

Bladder *stores urine until it is released*

Right ureter *carries urine from right kidney to bladder*

bladder wall

The stretchy wall of the bladder consists mainly of smooth muscle (above). This type of muscle works automatically without you noticing it, and contracts slowly and smoothly. You'll come across it in other organs, too, including the ureters.

reproductive system

Located in the same part of the body as the urinary system, male and female reproductive systems differ in structure, but both are involved in producing special cells that join up to make babies.

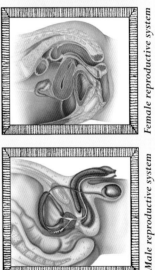

Male reproductive system

Female reproductive system

Teeth

Now we must provide our body-in-progress with the tools it needs to feed. Unlike snakes, humans can't swallow big chunks of food whole. That's why we need to install a set of teeth—ideal for chopping and crushing food into tiny pieces.

tooth types

The versatile dental toolkit consists of chisel-shaped incisors, pointed canines, and premolars and molars, both with ridges called cusps for chewing.

enamel

The hardest material in the body is white enamel. It must withstand the pressure, and wear and tear, of regular biting and chewing. Enamel doesn't contain cells or blood vessels so it cannot repair itself if it gets damaged.

Enamel consists of tightly packed rods of hard calcium phosphate

Canines grip, pierce, and tear food

Premolars aid molars in chewing food

Molars crush and grind food

Day 19

There's been a lot to chew over, but assistant and I have sunk our teeth into the material and gotten to the root of the matter. This is a taste of things to come tomorrow…

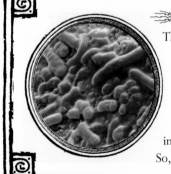

tooth bacteria

These bacteria live on the surface of a tooth. If you don't brush your teeth daily, bacteria and old food form a sticky mixture called plaque. The bacteria release acids as they feed, which can eat into enamel and cause tooth decay. So, brush those teeth!

Root of the tooth is firmly embedded in the jawbone

Crown of the tooth projects above the gum and makes contact with food

Wisdom teeth (back molars) are the last adult teeth to emerge

Incisors slice and chop food

firmly anchored

Beneath the white enamel crown are tooth-shaping dentine and a pulp cavity that contains nerves. These nerves allow you to "feel" chewing—and, sometimes, the pain of tooth decay. The roots of a tooth are held firmly in place in sockets in the upper and lower jawbones.

Enamel forms the white crown of the tooth

Gum forms tight collar around base of crown

Dentine supports the crown, and forms the root

Pulp cavity contains nerves and blood vessels

Periodontal ligament anchors tooth to socket in jawbone

Cementum binds tooth to periodontal ligament

Blood vessels supply the tooth with food and oxygen

full set

Humans have two sets of teeth during their lifetime. The first set of 20 baby teeth emerges from the jaws during childhood. These teeth are gradually replaced by adult teeth. A full adult set contains 16 teeth (six molars, four premolars, two canines, and four incisors) in each jaw.

Dentine is made from hard minerals

dentine

Bonelike dentine shapes a tooth and enables it to withstand the enormous pressure produced between the teeth when you chew. The cells that make and maintain dentine line the pulp cavity, and are kept alive by its blood supply.

Mouth, throat, and esophagus

Before we can put food inside the mouth, the body needs to be ready to make use of the food's nutrients. This process is called digestion. It occurs when food passes along a long tube called the alimentary canal, which begins with the mouth, throat, and esophagus.

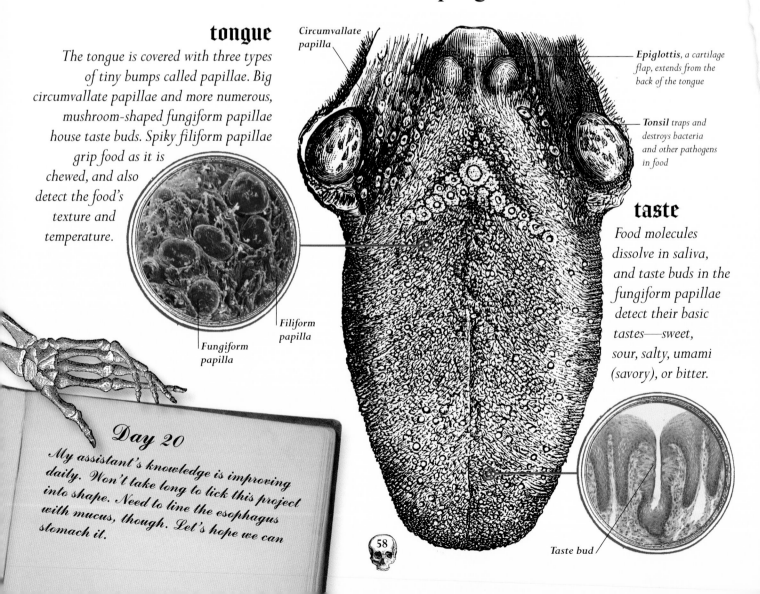

tongue

The tongue is covered with three types of tiny bumps called papillae. Big circumvallate papillae and more numerous, mushroom-shaped fungiform papillae house taste buds. Spiky filiform papillae grip food as it is chewed, and also detect the food's texture and temperature.

Circumvallate papilla

Filiform papilla

Fungiform papilla

Epiglottis, a cartilage flap, extends from the back of the tongue

Tonsil traps and destroys bacteria and other pathogens in food

taste

Food molecules dissolve in saliva, and taste buds in the fungiform papillae detect their basic tastes—sweet, sour, salty, umami (savory), or bitter.

Taste bud

Day 20

My assistant's knowledge is improving daily. Won't take long to lick this project into shape. Need to line the esophagus with mucus, though. Let's hope we can stomach it.

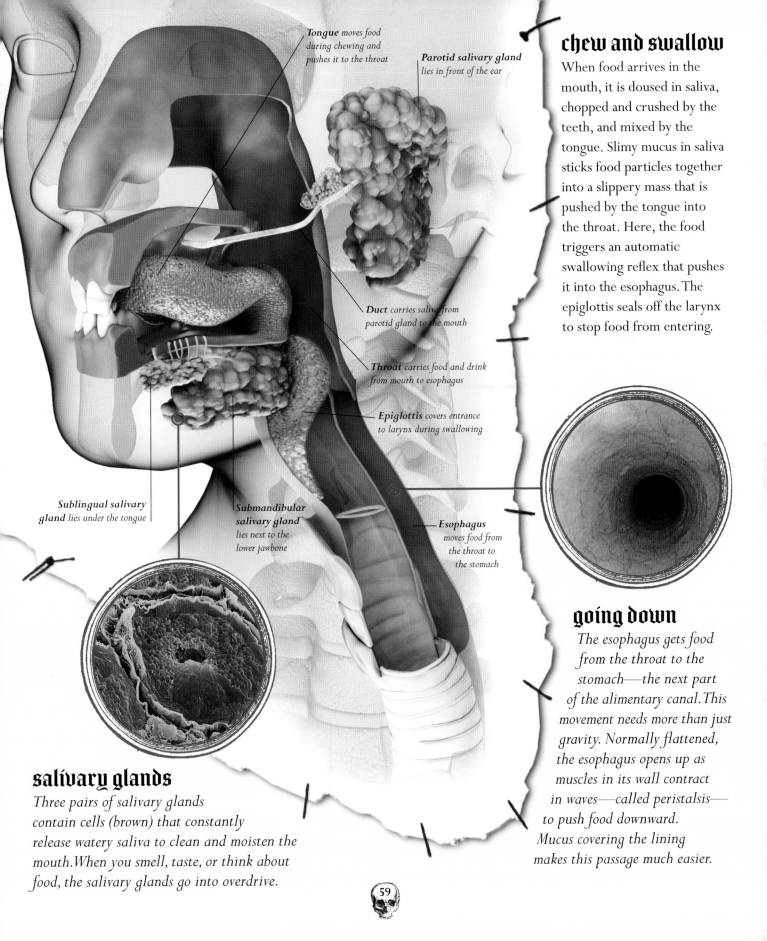

Tongue *moves food during chewing and pushes it to the throat*

Parotid salivary gland *lies in front of the ear*

Duct *carries saliva from parotid gland to the mouth*

Throat *carries food and drink from mouth to esophagus*

Epiglottis *covers entrance to larynx during swallowing*

Sublingual salivary gland *lies under the tongue*

Submandibular salivary gland *lies next to the lower jawbone*

Esophagus *moves food from the throat to the stomach*

chew and swallow

When food arrives in the mouth, it is doused in saliva, chopped and crushed by the teeth, and mixed by the tongue. Slimy mucus in saliva sticks food particles together into a slippery mass that is pushed by the tongue into the throat. Here, the food triggers an automatic swallowing reflex that pushes it into the esophagus. The epiglottis seals off the larynx to stop food from entering.

going down

The esophagus gets food from the throat to the stomach—the next part of the alimentary canal. This movement needs more than just gravity. Normally flattened, the esophagus opens up as muscles in its wall contract in waves—called peristalsis—to push food downward. Mucus covering the lining makes this passage much easier.

salivary glands

Three pairs of salivary glands contain cells (brown) that constantly release watery saliva to clean and moisten the mouth. When you smell, taste, or think about food, the salivary glands go into overdrive.

Stomach

Now it's time to install the stomach at the end of the esophagus. Here, swallowed food will be stored, liquidized, and released in small amounts to continue its journey down the alimentary canal.

gatekeeper

The pyloric sphincter is the stomach's own gatekeeper. This ring of muscle controls the flow of creamy, part-digested food from the stomach into the duodenum, the next part of the alimentary canal. It is usually contracted and closed, but relaxes and partially opens from time to time.

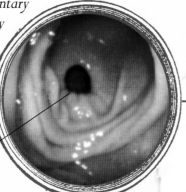

Pyloric sphincter *slightly open, showing the duodenum beyond*

folded lining

The volume of the stomach can increase from just 0.1 pints (50 ml) when empty, to a massive 8½ pints (4 liters), after a big meal. It can expand because of big folds in its lining.

Duodenum *is the first section of the small intestine*

muscular bag

The J-shaped stomach is the widest part of the alimentary canal. It is very elastic, and can expand enormously after a meal. It has three layers of smooth muscles in its wall—other parts of the alimentary canal only have two—to pummel food into a creamy paste called chyme.

Protective membrane
covers the stomach and other parts of the alimentary canal

Longitudinal muscle layer
runs the length of the stomach

Day 21
Assistant's appetite for the
information I churn out
has impressed me. I can't
stomach people who don't
want to learn. All this
talk about digestion has
got my gastric juices flowing.
My tummy's rumbling...
time for dinner.

Circular muscle layer
runs around the stomach

Oblique muscle layer
runs diagonally

Folds *in the lining of*
the stomach disappear
as it fills with food

Gastric pit *is opening*
in stomach lining that
leads to gastric gland

fill, churn, and empty

Even before food arrives, the sight or smell of food triggers the release of gastric juice. As food fills the expanding stomach, the nervous and hormonal systems control the churning of food, and its mixing with gastric juice, until the time comes for emptying.

1. Waves of muscular contraction, called peristalsis, pass through stomach wall, pushing newly arrived food away from the esophagus.

2. Vigorous contractions of the three layers of muscle churn food, mix it with gastric juice, and turn it into creamy chyme.

3. After a few hours of churning, chyme is liquid enough to be released in small squirts through the pyloric sphincter.

gastric glands

Millions of gastric glands in the stomach's lining release gastric juice. This contains powerful hydrochloric acid and the enzyme pepsin, which in acidic conditions part-digests proteins. A layer of mucus prevents the acid and enzyme from digesting the stomach itself.

Intestines

We finish off the alimentary canal by plumbing in the small and large intestines into a limited space inside the abdomen. It's here that the breakdown of major food groups—carbohydrates, fats, and proteins—into simple, usable nutrients is completed. Leftover waste is also removed.

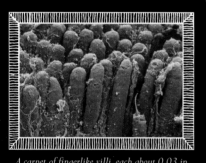

A carpet of fingerlike villi, each about 0.03 in (1 mm) long, lines the small intestine.

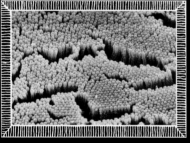

A mass of microvilli greatly increases the surface area of a villus cell for digestion and absorption.

villi

Each villus contains a blood capillary network that carries away glucose and amino acids, as well as lymph vessels that carry away fats. The cells that cover villi have their own microscopic projections, called microvilli.

small and large

The small intestine is the longest and most important part of the alimentary canal. Inside, digestion is completed and simple nutrients are absorbed. The shorter, but wider, large intestine—particularly the colon—forms and disposes of feces.

Duodenum *is the first part of the small intestine*

Circular folds *inside the small intestine covered by tiny villi*

huge surface

The small intestine has a massive surface area for digesting and absorbing. Circular folds in its lining provide a much bigger internal surface than a flat lining would do. The folds are covered by millions of villi, which carry some digestive enzymes. Others are provided by the pancreas. These enzymes complete the digestion of food into glucose, amino acids, and fatty acids, so that these nutrients can be absorbed into the blood.

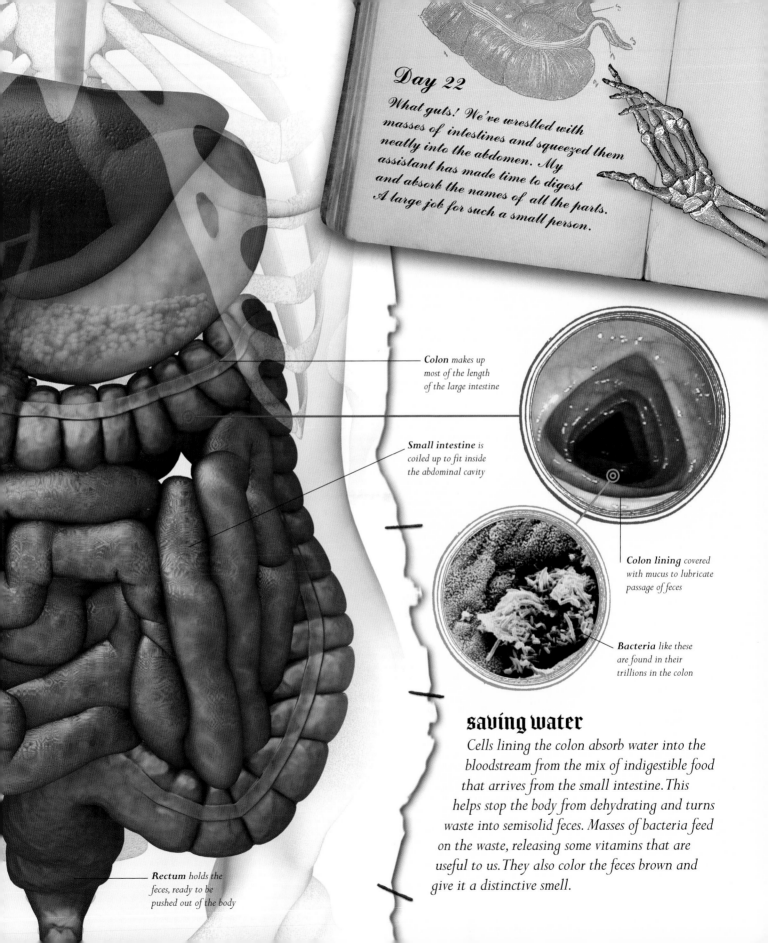

Day 22

What guts! We've wrestled with
masses of intestines and squeezed them
neatly into the abdomen. My
assistant has made time to digest
and absorb the names of all the parts.
A large job for such a small person.

Colon makes up
most of the length
of the large intestine

Small intestine is
coiled up to fit inside
the abdominal cavity

Colon lining covered
with mucus to lubricate
passage of feces

Bacteria like these
are found in their
trillions in the colon

Rectum holds the
feces, ready to be
pushed out of the body

saving water

Cells lining the colon absorb water into the
bloodstream from the mix of indigestible food
that arrives from the small intestine. This
helps stop the body from dehydrating and turns
waste into semisolid feces. Masses of bacteria feed
on the waste, releasing some vitamins that are
useful to us. They also color the feces brown and
give it a distinctive smell.

Liver and pancreas

Now it's time to insert the liver and pancreas. The liver takes up most of the space in the top of the abdomen, while the tadpole-shaped pancreas nestles beneath the stomach. Without the bile and pancreatic juice these two organs release, digestion wouldn't work properly.

Liver is the body's largest internal organ

Gall bladder stores bile

liver cells

These masters of multitasking perform more than 500 vital functions. In addition to making bile, liver cells process, store, and dispatch newly absorbed nutrients so that the right levels of these substances remain in the blood. They also rid the blood of poisonous chemicals.

Sheets of liver cells seen greatly magnified, surrounding large capillaries

Liver cells are arranged around branches of blood vessels

Gall bladder is tucked behind the liver

Duodenum receives bile and pancreatic juice

bile and juice

Both bile and pancreatic juice are released along ducts that merge before emptying into the duodenum. Made by the liver, bile is a mixture of bile salts, which play a part in fat digestion, and waste products. Pancreatic juice is produced by the pancreas and contains enzymes that break down fats, proteins, and carbohydrates in food into simpler substances.

Day 23

Today, assistant had the gall to ask me whether the liver is important. That certainly stirred up my juices! Of course it is, and so is the pancreas. Without them the digestive system just wouldn't be complete.

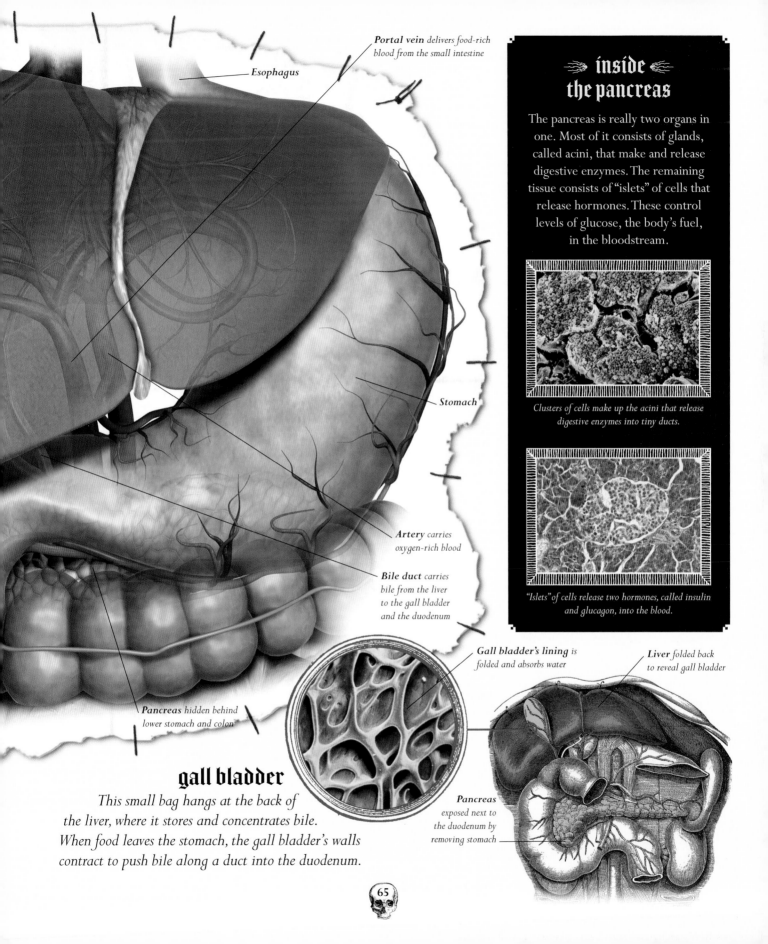

Esophagus

Portal vein *delivers food-rich blood from the small intestine*

Stomach

Artery *carries oxygen-rich blood*

Bile duct *carries bile from the liver to the gall bladder and the duodenum*

Pancreas *hidden behind lower stomach and colon*

ᚐ inside ᚐ the pancreas

The pancreas is really two organs in one. Most of it consists of glands, called acini, that make and release digestive enzymes. The remaining tissue consists of "islets" of cells that release hormones. These control levels of glucose, the body's fuel, in the bloodstream.

Clusters of cells make up the acini that release digestive enzymes into tiny ducts.

"Islets" of cells release two hormones, called insulin and glucagon, into the blood.

Gall bladder's lining *is folded and absorbs water*

Liver *folded back to reveal gall bladder*

Pancreas *exposed next to the duodenum by removing stomach*

gall bladder

This small bag hangs at the back of the liver, where it stores and concentrates bile. When food leaves the stomach, the gall bladder's walls contract to push bile along a duct into the duodenum.

Digestive system

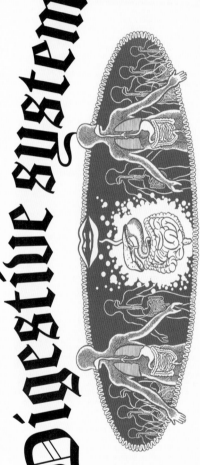

At last, we've assembled all the sections of the alimentary canal, and added the liver and pancreas to make the digestive system. Its job is to break down the big molecules in food into small molecules that the body can use.

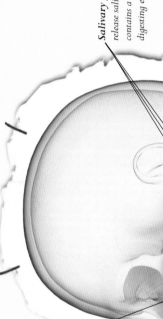

chemical digesters

Digestion would be impossible without enzymes. These chemical digesters increase (by thousands or millions of times) the rate at which food is broken down into nutrients. This enzyme (above), called pepsin, is released into the stomach to break down proteins.

food processor

Whether it's starchy carbohydrates in pasta, proteins in fish, or fats in peanuts, your digestive system can process it. Food is crushed and churned by the teeth and stomach walls. Enzyme action in the mouth, stomach, and small intestine converts crushed food into simple nutrients —glucose, amino acids, and fatty acids—perfect for energy, growth, and repair.

Salivary glands release saliva, which contains a starch-digesting enzyme

Food is chewed, crushed, and mixed with saliva in the mouth

Food takes 10 seconds to travel down the esophagus from throat to stomach

Stomach churns food for about three hours—more if it contains lots of fat

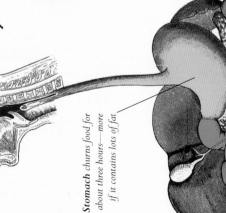

Small intestine takes about six hours to complete digestion

Watery waste is dried out to form feces after 12 to 36 hours in the large intestine

slow process

The alimentary canal is about 29 ft (9 m) from mouth to anus. It takes hours for food to be pushed along the canal by muscular movement, but that allows plenty of time for food to be completely digested and absorbed.

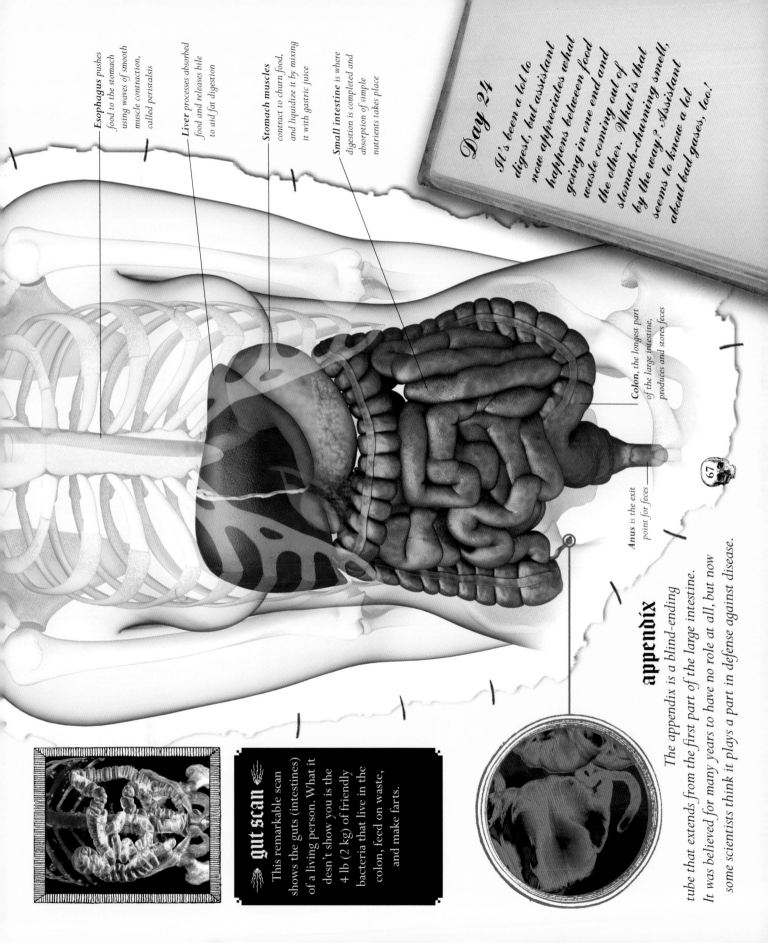

Esophagus *pushes food to the stomach using waves of smooth muscle contraction, called peristalsis*

Liver *processes absorbed food and releases bile to aid fat digestion*

Stomach muscles *contract to churn food, and liquidize it by mixing it with gastric juice*

Small intestine *is where digestion is completed and absorption of simple nutrients takes place*

Colon, *the longest part of the large intestine, produces and stores feces*

Anus *is the exit point for feces*

Day 24

It's been a lot to digest, but assistant now appreciates what happens between food going in one end and waste coming out of the other. What is that stomach-churning smell, by the way? Assistant seems to know a lot about bad gases, too!

67

gut scan

This remarkable scan shows the guts (intestines) of a living person. What it doesn't show you is the 4 lb (2 kg) of friendly bacteria that live in the colon, feed on waste, and make farts.

appendix

The appendix is a blind-ending tube that extends from the first part of the large intestine. It was believed for many years to have no role at all, but now some scientists think it plays a part in defense against disease.

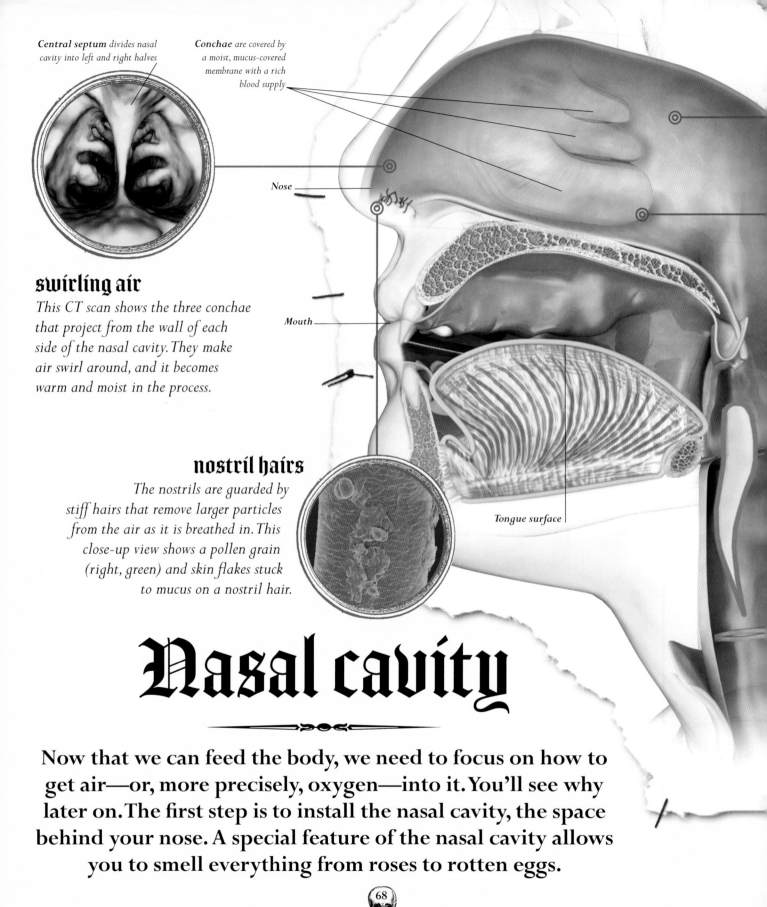

Central septum *divides nasal cavity into left and right halves*

Conchae *are covered by a moist, mucus-covered membrane with a rich blood supply*

Nose

Mouth

Tongue surface

swirling air

This CT scan shows the three conchae that project from the wall of each side of the nasal cavity. They make air swirl around, and it becomes warm and moist in the process.

nostril hairs

The nostrils are guarded by stiff hairs that remove larger particles from the air as it is breathed in. This close-up view shows a pollen grain (right, green) and skin flakes stuck to mucus on a nostril hair.

Nasal cavity

Now that we can feed the body, we need to focus on how to get air—or, more precisely, oxygen—into it. You'll see why later on. The first step is to install the nasal cavity, the space behind your nose. A special feature of the nasal cavity allows you to smell everything from roses to rotten eggs.

smell detectors

At the top of each side of the nasal cavity is a patch of lining called the olfactory (smell) epithelium. Within it are odor receptor cells. These respond when smell molecules in the air dissolve in the watery mucus that covers them.

stick and waft

Some cells lining the nasal cavity produce sticky mucus. Others have hairlike cilia on their outer surfaces. Particles and pathogens in the swirling air stick to the mucus. Cilia sway backward and forward to waft dirt-laden mucus to the throat, where it is swallowed and digested.

Cilia in the nasal cavity lining move mucus

inside the nose

The nasal cavity is a wind tunnel that carries air from the two nostrils to the throat. En route, the air is warmed, moistened, and filtered to remove particles and pathogens that might cause damage deeper inside the body.

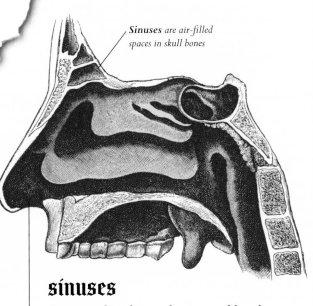

Sinuses are air-filled spaces in skull bones

sinuses

Connected to the nasal cavity and lined with the same moist membrane, sinuses serve to make the skull lighter. They also help to moisten and warm air, and make our voices sound the way they do.

Nostrils are the entrances to nasal cavity

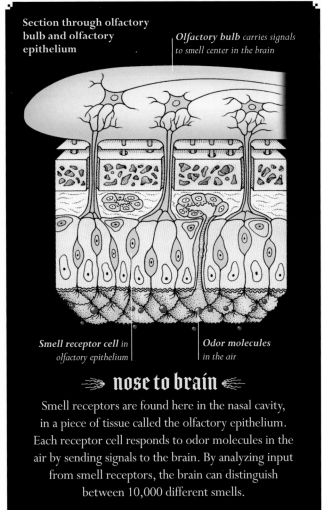

Section through olfactory bulb and olfactory epithelium

Olfactory bulb carries signals to smell center in the brain

Smell receptor cell in olfactory epithelium

Odor molecules in the air

⇒ nose to brain ⇐

Smell receptors are found here in the nasal cavity, in a piece of tissue called the olfactory epithelium. Each receptor cell responds to odor molecules in the air by sending signals to the brain. By analyzing input from smell receptors, the brain can distinguish between 10,000 different smells.

Larynx, trachea, and bronchi

It's time to install and connect the airways. Where did I put that pile of tubes? The trachea and bronchi are straightforward. It's when the bronchi start branching out into the lungs that things get more complicated.

voice box

The funnellike larynx links the throat and trachea and is made of several pieces of cartilage. In addition to being an air passage, the larynx also contains the sound-producing vocal cords, hence its alternative name—the voice box.

Cricoid cartilage is anchored to the top of the trachea

Thyroid cartilage bulges out at the front to form the Adam's apple

windpipe

Look down the trachea, or windpipe, of a living person and you'll see its pink lining covered with slimy mucus. Those ridges are formed by C-shaped cartilage rings, which stop the trachea from collapsing inward when air whooshes through it.

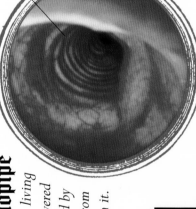

Cartilage rings keep the trachea open as air moves through it

airways

These tubes carry air into and out of the chest. At the base of the throat, the larynx leads to the trachea, which branches into two bronchi. These divide many times to form tiny bronchioles. It's like an upside-down "tree," with the trachea as the trunk, bronchi as branches, and bronchioles as twigs.

Trachea is a flexible tube that links larynx to bronchi

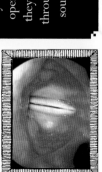

making sounds

Two membranes, the vocal cords, cross the larynx. Normally, they're open. When they close, they vibrate as air passes through them, producing sounds that are turned into speech.

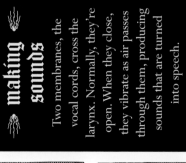

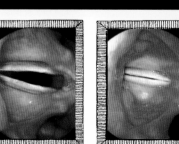

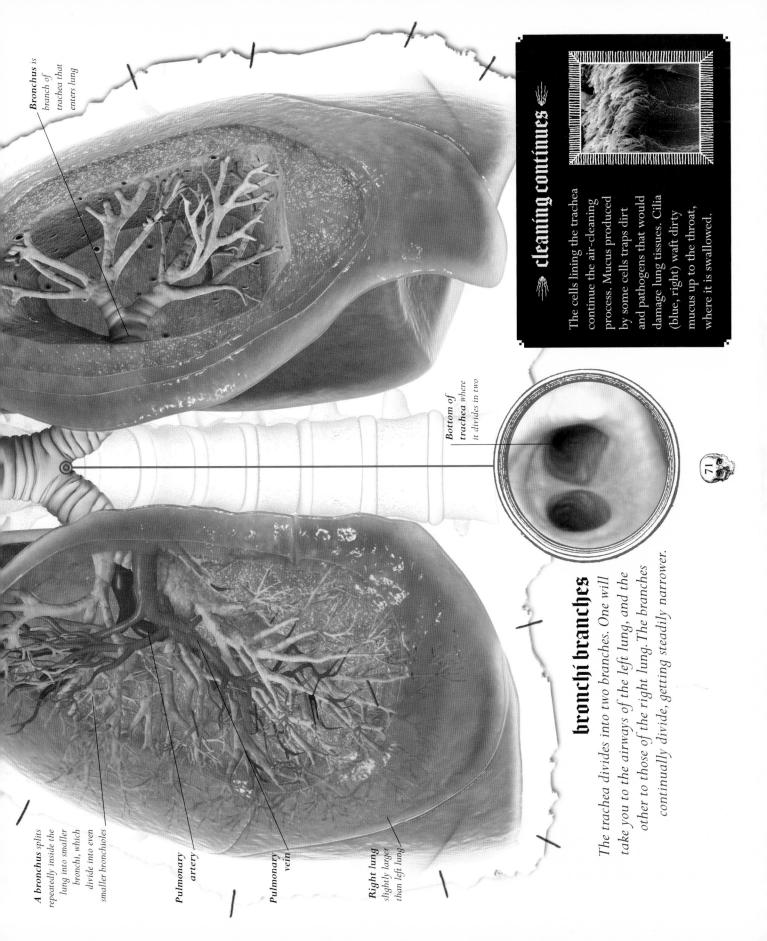

Bronchus is branch of trachea that enters lung

cleaning continues

The cells lining the trachea continue the air-cleaning process. Mucus produced by some cells traps dirt and pathogens that would damage lung tissues. Cilia (blue, right) waft dirty mucus up to the throat, where it is swallowed.

Bottom of trachea where it divides in two

bronchi branches

The trachea divides into two branches. One will take you to the airways of the left lung, and the other to those of the right lung. The branches continually divide, getting steadily narrower.

A bronchus splits repeatedly inside the lung into smaller bronchi, which divide into even smaller bronchioles

Pulmonary artery

Pulmonary vein

Right lung slightly larger than left lung

Lungs

At the center of the respiratory system are the lungs. Packed with air-filled passages and bags, these two spongy organs play a vital part in helping to exchange oxygen for unwanted carbon dioxide. Take a deep breath and let's get started.

Terminal bronchiole is no wider than a hair on your head

Right lung is divided into three lobes

chest fillers

Filling most of the space inside the chest, the lungs surround the heart. Blood travels a short distance from the heart to the lungs to pick up oxygen, then back to the heart to be pumped to body cells.

Heart is surrounded by the two lungs

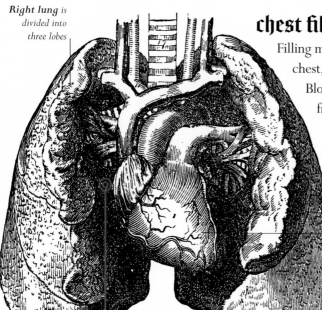

Branching bronchi and bronchioles shown in X-ray of a lung

Elastic fibers

bronchi to bronchioles

The single bronchus entering each lung divides into smaller bronchi that branch into even smaller bronchi. These small bronchi split into tiny tubes called bronchioles. The smallest branches of bronchioles end in the alveoli.

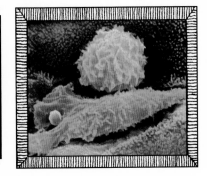

≫ rib protection

Assisted by the backbone and sternum (breastbone), 12 pairs of ribs form a protective cage. They surround the lungs as well as the heart and major blood vessels that we've already installed. And, as you'll soon find out, the ribs play a key part in breathing.

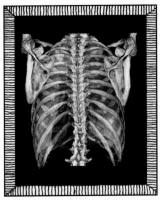

CT scan of chest from the rear showing lungs (blue) surrounded by ribs.

Alveoli are arranged into bunches like grapes

air bags

The finest bronchiole branches lead to air bags called alveoli. Through their moist linings, oxygen from the air passes into the bloodstream, while waste carbon dioxide passes in the opposite direction. Together, the 300 million alveoli in both lungs provide a massive surface area for this exchange of gases.

Branch of pulmonary artery *delivers oxygen-poor blood*

Capillary network *surrounds alveoli*

Branch of pulmonary vein *takes away oxygen-rich blood*

Day 25
Breathtaking progress today. I refused to leave everything up in the air and covered the lungs in detail. Assistant was blown away.

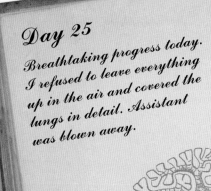

73

Respiratory system

Our complete respiratory system gets oxygen into the body and removes carbon dioxide. Cells need a nonstop supply of oxygen to release the energy that keeps them alive. They also need to get rid of waste carbon dioxide. For all this to happen, air must be moved in and out of the lungs by breathing.

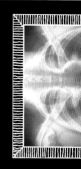

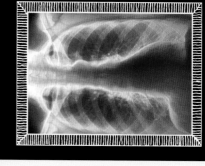

An X-ray of inhalation shows the ribs, lungs (blue), and diaphragm (orange).

Air turbulence caused by a sneeze is revealed in this special photograph.

sneezing

Irritations in the nasal cavity are removed by sneezing. Air builds up behind the vocal cords and is suddenly released. This blasts air at high speed through the nasal passages and out through the nostrils.

getting oxygen

The lungs are passive "bags" that cannot expand and shrink of their own accord. Getting air into and out of the lungs involves the diaphragm and intercostal muscles. Their activities result in inhalation (breathing in) and exhalation (breathing out).

Nasal cavity *warms, moistens, and filters air*

Epiglottis *prevents food entering larynx during swallowing*

Larynx *contains vocal cords, which produce sound*

Esophagus *lies behind trachea and carries food to the stomach*

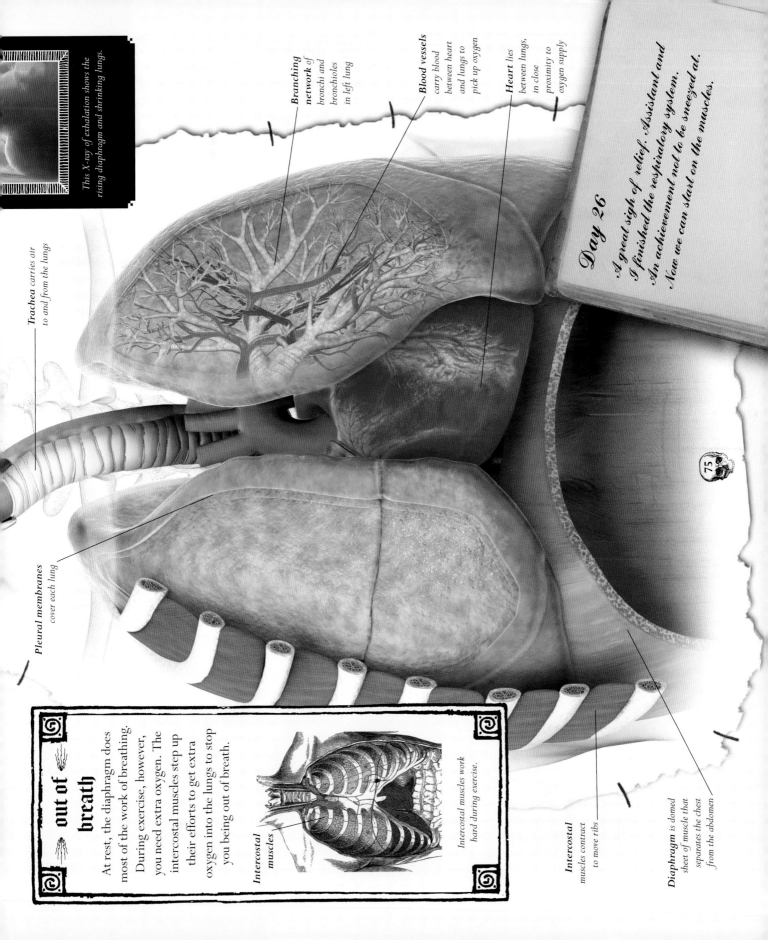

This X-ray of exhalation shows the rising diaphragm and shrinking lungs.

Trachea carries air to and from the lungs

Pleural membranes cover each lung

Branching network of bronchi and bronchioles in left lung

Blood vessels carry blood between heart and lungs to pick up oxygen

Heart lies between lungs, in close proximity to oxygen supply

Day 26

A great sigh of relief. Assistant and I finished the respiratory system. An achievement not to be sneezed at. Now we can start on the muscles.

75

out of breath

At rest, the diaphragm does most of the work of breathing. During exercise, however, you need extra oxygen. The intercostal muscles step up their efforts to get extra oxygen into the lungs to stop you being out of breath.

Intercostal muscles

Intercostal muscles work hard during exercise.

Intercostal muscles contract to move ribs

Diaphragm is domed sheet of muscle that separates the chest from the abdomen

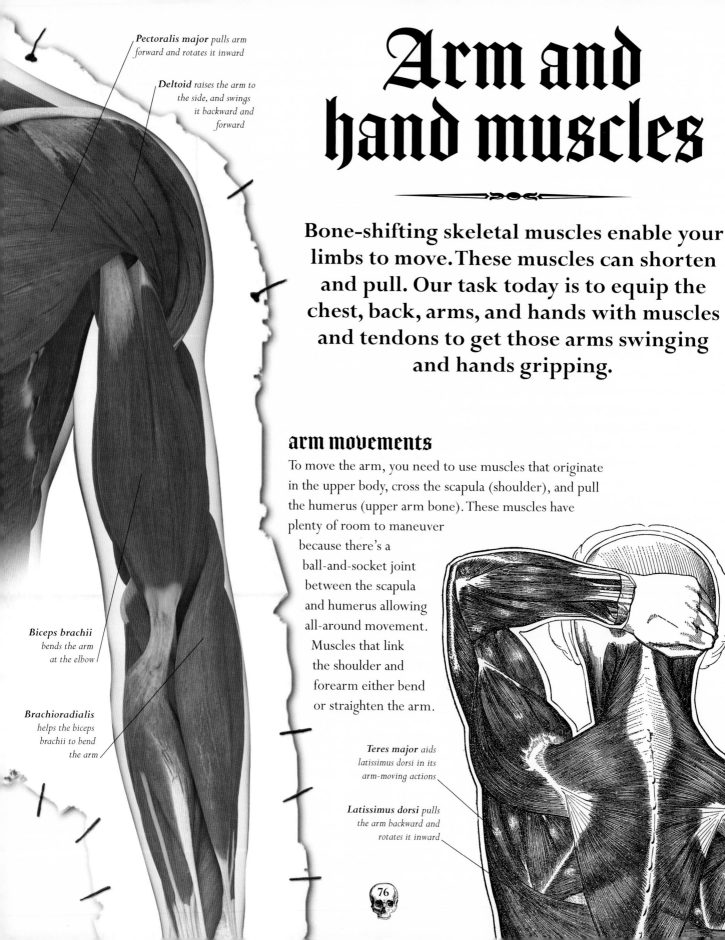

Arm and hand muscles

Bone-shifting skeletal muscles enable your limbs to move. These muscles can shorten and pull. Our task today is to equip the chest, back, arms, and hands with muscles and tendons to get those arms swinging and hands gripping.

Pectoralis major *pulls arm forward and rotates it inward*

Deltoid *raises the arm to the side, and swings it backward and forward*

Biceps brachii *bends the arm at the elbow*

Brachioradialis *helps the biceps brachii to bend the arm*

arm movements

To move the arm, you need to use muscles that originate in the upper body, cross the scapula (shoulder), and pull the humerus (upper arm bone). These muscles have plenty of room to maneuver because there's a ball-and-socket joint between the scapula and humerus allowing all-around movement. Muscles that link the shoulder and forearm either bend or straighten the arm.

Teres major *aids latissimus dorsi in its arm-moving actions*

Latissimus dorsi *pulls the arm backward and rotates it inward*

wrist and fingers

Many of the hand's movements are produced by forearm muscles. Most muscles in the inner forearm bend the wrist and fingers. Those in the outer forearm generally straighten the wrist and fingers. Note that the forearm muscles are attached to the hand bones by very long tendons.

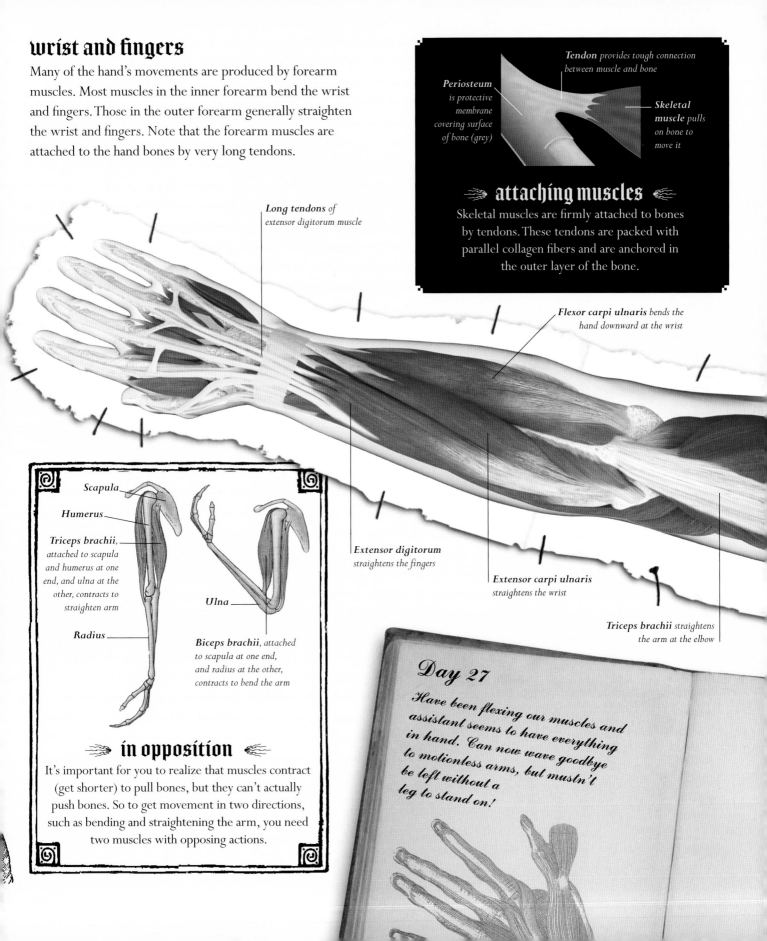

Tendon provides tough connection between muscle and bone

Periosteum is protective membrane covering surface of bone (grey)

Skeletal muscle pulls on bone to move it

attaching muscles

Skeletal muscles are firmly attached to bones by tendons. These tendons are packed with parallel collagen fibers and are anchored in the outer layer of the bone.

Long tendons of extensor digitorum muscle

Flexor carpi ulnaris bends the hand downward at the wrist

Extensor digitorum straightens the fingers

Extensor carpi ulnaris straightens the wrist

Triceps brachii straightens the arm at the elbow

Scapula

Humerus

Triceps brachii, attached to scapula and humerus at one end, and ulna at the other, contracts to straighten arm

Radius

Ulna

Biceps brachii, attached to scapula at one end, and radius at the other, contracts to bend the arm

in opposition

It's important for you to realize that muscles contract (get shorter) to pull bones, but they can't actually push bones. So to get movement in two directions, such as bending and straightening the arm, you need two muscles with opposing actions.

Day 27

Have been flexing our muscles and assistant seems to have everything in hand. Can now wave goodbye to motionless arms, but mustn't be left without a leg to stand on!

Hip and leg muscles

Ready to move on to the big muscles? Many hip and thigh muscles are bulky because they have to support and move the whole body when you walk or run. Lower leg muscles are powerful, too. Try standing on tiptoe and you can feel your calf muscles at work.

hip and thigh

Thigh muscles are attached to the hip bones at one end, and the femur or lower leg bones at the other. Muscles at the front of the thigh bend the thigh at the hip. The quadriceps femoris also straightens the knee. Muscles at the back of the thigh straighten the thigh at the hip. The hamstrings also bend the knee.

Tensor fasciae latae bends the thigh at the hip and rotates inward

Adductor longus pulls and rotates the thigh inward

Sartorius bends the thigh at the hip and pulls it outward

Iliopsoas consists of two muscles that bend the thigh at the hip

Pectineus pulls the thigh inward and bends it at the hip

Gluteus medius pulls the thigh out to the side and rotates it inward

Gluteus maximus (shown cut) straightens the thigh at the hip

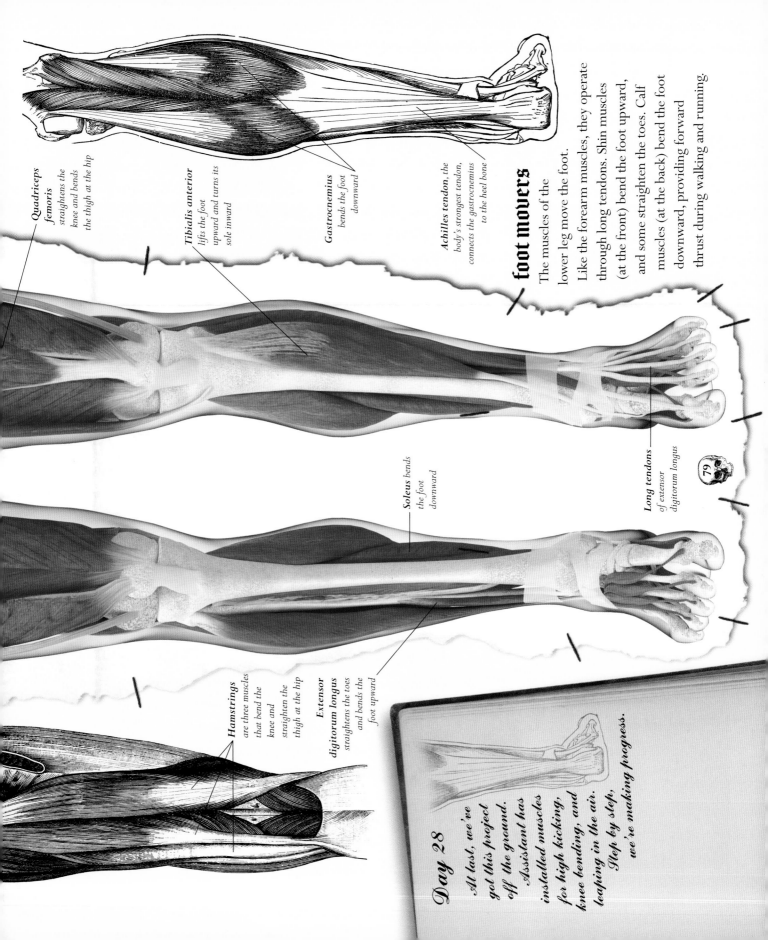

Quadriceps femoris *straightens the knee and bends the thigh at the hip*

Tibialis anterior *lifts the foot upward and turns its sole inward*

Gastrocnemius *bends the foot downward*

Achilles tendon, *the body's strongest tendon, connects the gastrocnemius to the heel bone*

foot movers

The muscles of the lower leg move the foot. Like the forearm muscles, they operate through long tendons. Shin muscles (at the front) bend the foot upward, and some straighten the toes. Calf muscles (at the back) bend the foot downward, providing forward thrust during walking and running.

Soleus *bends the foot downward*

Long tendons *of extensor digitorum longus*

Hamstrings *are three muscles that bend the knee and straighten the thigh at the hip*

Extensor digitorum longus *straightens the toes and bends the foot upward*

79

Day 28

At last, we've got this project off the ground. Assistant has installed muscles for high kicking, knee bending, and leaping in the air. Step by step, we're making progress.

Head and neck muscles

Our body may be moving, but it hasn't got much of an expression on its face! That will change when we install some facial muscles. Once we get the eyes moving and the jaws chomping, it will be all smiles.

making faces

About 30 facial muscles produce the variety of expressions that communicate our thoughts and emotions. Attached to skull bones, these muscles are unusual because they don't pull bones, but instead tug the skin of the face.

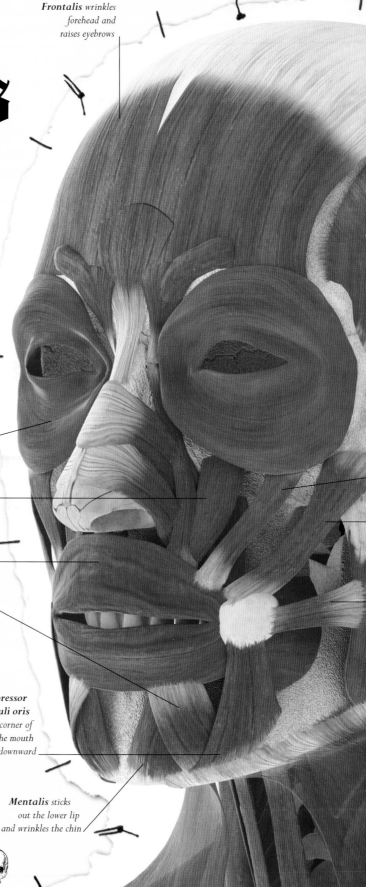

Frontalis *wrinkles forehead and raises eyebrows*

Orbicularis oculi *closes the eye*

Levator labii superioris *raises and curls the upper lip*

Orbicularis oris *purses the lips*

Depressor labii inferioris *pulls lower lip downward*

Depressor anguli oris *pulls corner of the mouth downward*

Mentalis *sticks out the lower lip and wrinkles the chin*

facial expressions

Whether you're smiling or frowning, or looking sad, angry, or surprised, people anywhere in the world can understand what you are feeling from the expression on your face.

Galea aponeurotica *connects frontalis to scalp-pulling muscle*

Superior oblique *swivels eye outward and downward*

Superior rectus

Medial rectus

Lateral rectus

eye movers

Six muscles anchored to the eye socket move each eyeball. Four rectus muscles move the eye up (superior), down (inferior), inward (medial), or outward (lateral). Two oblique muscles swivel the eye diagonally. All six produce very precise movements so you can follow objects as they go by.

Inferior oblique *swivels eye outward and upward*

Inferior rectus

Temporalis *pulls lower jaw upward*

⇒ jaw muscles ⇐

Together, the masseter and temporalis create the massive crushing force used by the teeth to bite. With the help of some smaller muscles, they also help you to chew and grind your food.

Temporalis *pulls the lower jaw upward*

Masseter *has same action as temporalis*

Zygomaticus minor *raises the upper lip*

Zygomaticus major *raises corner of mouth upward into a smile*

Risorius *pulls corner of lip to the side when smiling*

Sternocleidomastoid *bends head forward and to the side*

muscle fibers

These are the long, cylindrical fibers (cells, left) that are bundled together to make a skeletal muscle. Give them a fuel and oxygen—to supply energy—and stimulate them with an electrical nerve signal, and they will contract. The end result is a muscle movement, such as a wink or a grin.

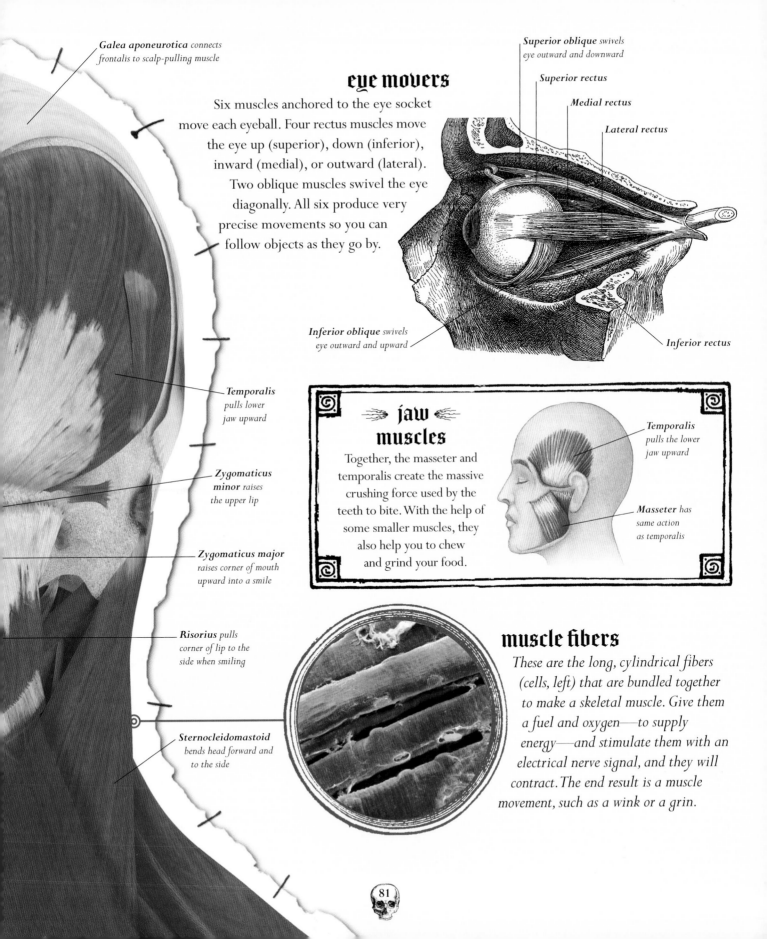

Muscular System

Skeletal muscles

If you could count them all, there would be about 650 bone-pulling skeletal muscles in our new creation. They are arranged——as you can see below——in layers ranging from deep to superficial (surface). Muscle names are in Latin and describe a muscle's size, shape, location, or job.

Orbicularis oculi *closes the eyelids*

Zygomaticus *makes you smile*

Deltoid *raises arm sideways and swings it backward and forward*

Biceps brachii *bends the arm at the elbow*

how muscles work

The long, cylindrical fibers, or cells, that make up muscles have a highly organized structure. Each fiber is packed with parallel, rodlike myofibrils. They contain arrays of filaments arranged in a way that gives myofibrils a striped appearance. The filaments interact to make myofibrils, fibers, and the muscle contract.

Now that we have the muscular system in place, you can really see the body shaping up. Remember, though, that these muscles do more than just shape and move us. They also help stabilize joints, hold us upright so we don't collapse in a heap, and release heat to keep our insides warm.

Myofibrils *running in parallel (left to right) in this section along a muscle fiber*

Triceps brachii *straightens the arm at the elbow*

Trapezius *pulls the shoulders and head backward*

Splenius capitis *pulls head backward, turns it to one side, and keeps it upright*

Occipitalis *pulls the scalp backward*

Pectoralis major *pulls arm forward and toward the body*

Sternocleidomastoid *bends head forward and turns it to one side*

Frontalis *raises the eyebrows and wrinkles the forehead*

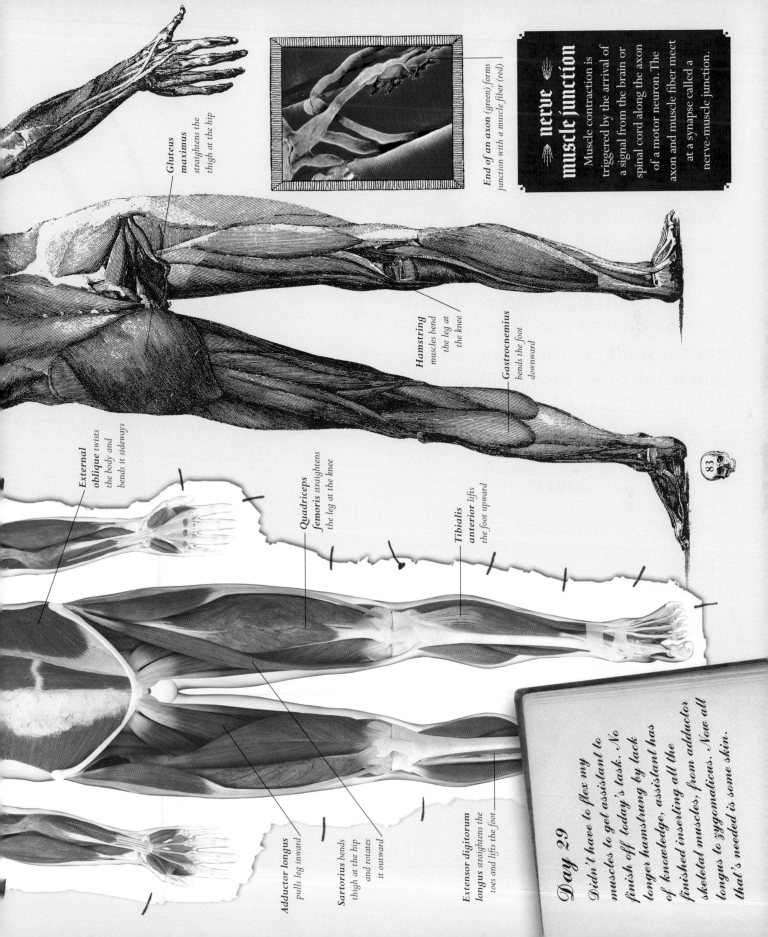

Gluteus maximus *straightens the thigh at the hip*

End of an axon *(green) forms junction with a muscle fiber (red)*

Hamstring *muscles bend the leg at the knee*

Gastrocnemius *bends the foot downward*

External oblique *twists the body and bends it sideways*

Quadriceps femoris *straightens the leg at the knee*

Tibialis anterior *lifts the foot upward*

83

Adductor longus *pulls leg inward*

Sartorius *bends thigh at the hip and rotates it outward*

Extensor digitorum longus *straightens the toes and lifts the foot*

Day 29

Didn't have to flex my muscles to get assistant to finish off today's task. No longer hamstrung by lack of knowledge, assistant has finished inserting all the skeletal muscles, from adductor longus to zygomaticus. Now all that's needed is some skin.

Skin, hair, and nails

Now we must cover our body with skin to protect its delicate tissues. This living overcoat is flexible, self-repairing, waterproof, and germ-proof. It also filters harmful rays in sunlight. Your skin can sense touch, pressure, heat, cold, and pain. It also helps the body to maintain a steady internal temperature.

two layers

The epidermis, the skin's upper layer, is its protective part. Its uppermost cells are packed with the waterproof protein keratin, also found in hair and nails. The dermis, the lower, thicker layer, has a blood supply, sweat glands, nerves, sensory endings, and hair follicles.

☙ hot or cold? ❧
When your body is hot, sweat glands release sweat that evaporates, draws heat from your body, and cools you. At the same time, dermis blood vessels widen to release more heat. If you're cold, sweating stops, blood vessels narrow, and you retain heat.

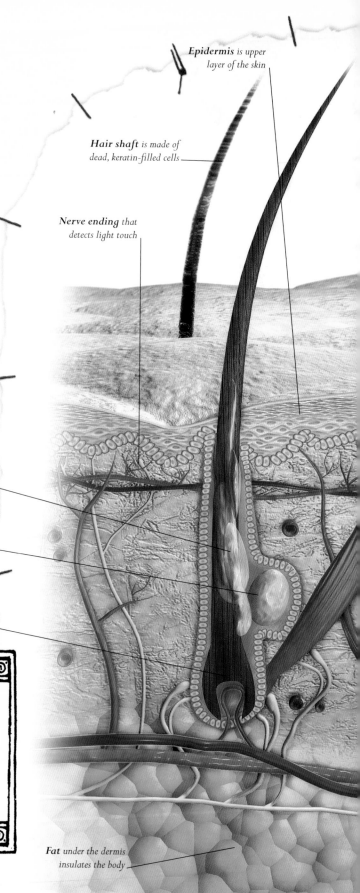

Epidermis is upper layer of the skin

Hair shaft is made of dead, keratin-filled cells

Nerve ending that detects light touch

Hair follicle is cavity from which hair grows

Sebaceous gland produces oily sebum

Hair bulb contains living cells that divide to make hair grow

Fat under the dermis insulates the body

germ protection

Skin provides a vital barrier against infection by microorganisms. Bacteria live harmlessly on your skin, but if the epidermis is cut, they can invade the dermis and bloodstream and cause harm. Fortunately, as the skin repairs itself, the body's defenses attack the invaders.

Staphylococcus epidermidis bacteria *living on the skin*

Sweat droplet *emerges from sweat pore— opening of sweat gland*

Skin flakes *surround a sweat pore*

skin flakes

The surface layers of the epidermis are formed from dead, flattened cells filled with keratin. These cells are constantly worn away as skin flakes, and replaced by the division of living cells deeper in the epidermis.

Nerve ending *that detects heat, cold, or pain*

Dermis *containing blood vessels, glands, and nerve endings*

Muscle *that pulls hair upright and produces goosebumps*

Artery *supplies oxygen-rich blood to dermis*

Sweat gland *makes and releases sweat*

⇒ hard as nails ⇐

Ideal for scratching itches and gripping small objects, nails consist of dead, flattened cells like these (above). A nail grows from living cells at its base, which die as they move forward and fill with tough keratin.

The complete body

Congratulations! With your invaluable help, we've managed to assemble a complete living, breathing human being. Let's reflect on this fantastic achievement. We'll take a look at the parts we've assembled and run some tests to check that everything's working.

Brain controls body activities and enables us to feel, move, and think

Kidneys remove waste and excess water from the blood to make urine, which is then released

Lungs get essential oxygen into the bloodstream and remove waste carbon dioxide

Liver aids digestion, stores nutrients, and processes blood to regulate its composition

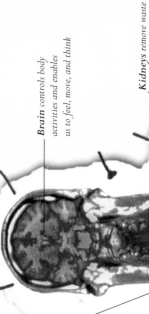

whole body scan

There's no need to pull the body apart to review the organs that we've added. Instead, this remarkable MRI scan shows the insides of the human body. You can see some of the body's major components, including bones, muscles, lungs, and the brain.

System check

Earlier you discovered that tissues make organs, and organs link up to form 12 body systems. Now the systems are in place, you need to remember that they work together. For example, the circulatory system supplies every organ with oxygen and food obtained by the respiratory and digestive systems.

Circulatory system *transports the food and oxygen cells need to release energy*

Respiratory system *ensures oxygen gets into the bloodstream*

Digestive system *breaks down food into nutrients that can be used by cells*

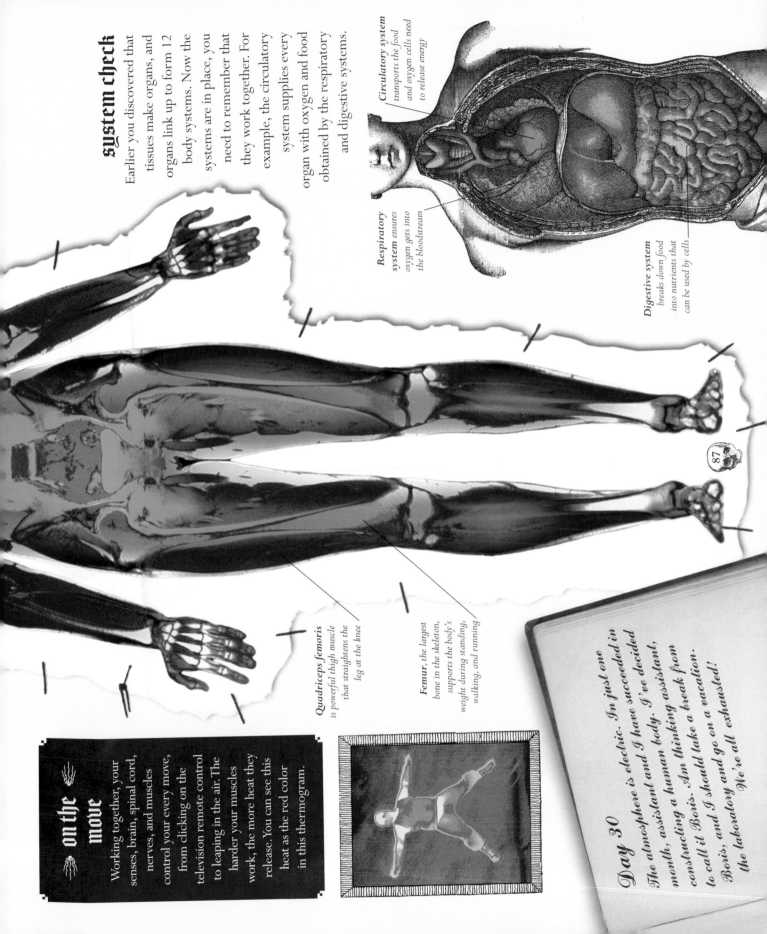

Quadriceps femoris *is powerful thigh muscle that straightens the leg at the knee*

Femur, *the largest bone in the skeleton, supports the body's weight during standing, walking, and running*

On the move

Working together, your senses, brain, spinal cord, nerves, and muscles control your every move, from clicking on the television remote control to leaping in the air. The harder your muscles work, the more heat they release. You can see this heat as the red color in this thermogram.

Day 30
The atmosphere is electric. In just one month, assistant and I have succeeded in constructing a human body. Am thinking assistant, to call it Boris. Am thinking I should take a break from Boris, and go on a vacation. Boris and I are all exhausted! the laboratory. We're all exhausted!

Seeing inside

Throughout this project I have used various techniques—some old, some new—to check on the structure and workings of cells, tissues, and organs. You will have seen X-rays, angiograms, and MRI scans among the variety of images. Now I've got a little time to explain how these images are produced.

X-ray machine

When X-rays were discovered in 1895 by Wilhelm Roentgen, they had an immediate impact. For the first time, doctors could see bones without cutting open the body. X-rays are still used in hospitals today.

Vacuum tube *produces X-rays*

Cable *carries electricity to vacuum tube*

Early X-ray showing Mrs. Roentgen's finger bones and a ring.

Early X-ray machine *attached to adjustable framework*

Handle *adjusts height and angle of vacuum tube*

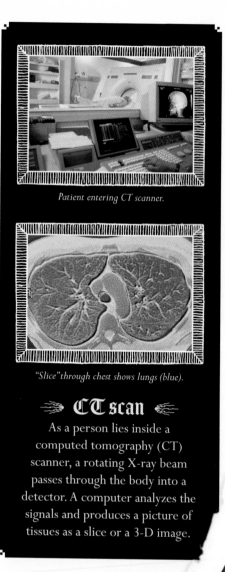

Patient entering CT scanner.

"Slice" through chest shows lungs (blue).

CT scan

As a person lies inside a computed tomography (CT) scanner, a rotating X-ray beam passes through the body into a detector. A computer analyzes the signals and produces a picture of tissues as a slice or a 3-D image.

88

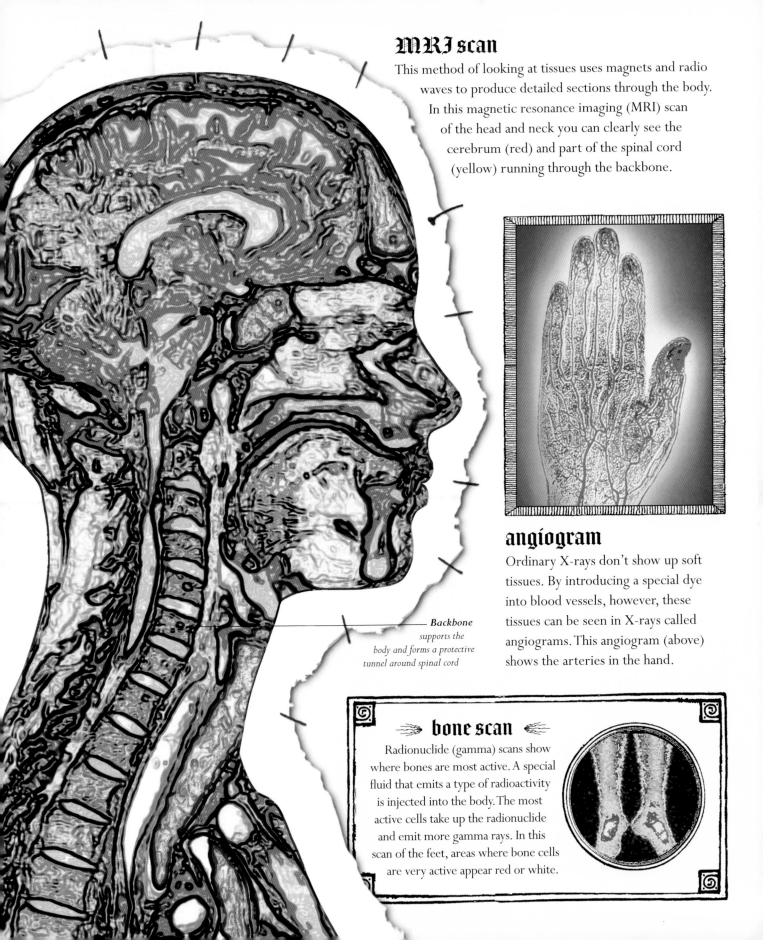

MRI scan

This method of looking at tissues uses magnets and radio waves to produce detailed sections through the body. In this magnetic resonance imaging (MRI) scan of the head and neck you can clearly see the cerebrum (red) and part of the spinal cord (yellow) running through the backbone.

Backbone
supports the body and forms a protective tunnel around spinal cord

angiogram

Ordinary X-rays don't show up soft tissues. By introducing a special dye into blood vessels, however, these tissues can be seen in X-rays called angiograms. This angiogram (above) shows the arteries in the hand.

bone scan

Radionuclide (gamma) scans show where bones are most active. A special fluid that emits a type of radioactivity is injected into the body. The most active cells take up the radionuclide and emit more gamma rays. In this scan of the feet, areas where bone cells are very active appear red or white.

Glossary

abdomen
The part of the body between the chest and the hips.

alimentary canal
The tube that extends from the mouth to the anus.

antibody
A substance released by the immune system that marks a pathogen.

artery
A blood vessel that carries blood away from the heart toward the tissues.

atom
The smallest part of a pure substance.

atrium
One of two upper heart chambers.

autonomic nervous system
The part of the nervous system that automatically controls certain activities, such as heart rate and sweating.

axon
A long, thin part extending from a neuron that carries nerve signals to another neuron.

bacteria
Microorganisms that can cause disease.

carbon dioxide
A gas released by cells as a waste product.

cardiac muscle
A type of muscle found only in the heart.

cartilage
A type of connective tissue that supports the body.

cell
One of the many microscopic living units from which the body is built.

cerebral cortex
The surface layer of the cerebrum, the largest part of the brain.

dendrite
A short process that extends from a neuron and receives signals from other neurons.

digestion
The breakdown of complex molecules in food into simple nutrients that can be used by the body.

DNA (deoxyribonucleic acid)
A molecule found inside the nucleus of a cell that carries instructions (genes) on how the cell should work.

endocrine system
A collection of glands that release hormones into the bloodstream.

enzyme
A protein that accelerates the rate of chemical reactions.

fat
A substance that supplies energy and insulates the body.

feces
The semisolid waste left at the end of digestion.

gland
A group of cells that produce and release substances.

glucose
A sugar that is the main source of energy for body cells.

hormone
A chemical messenger released by an endocrine gland to control certain body activities.

immune system
The system of defense cells that track and destroy pathogens to protect the body against disease.

joint
A place where two or more bones meet.

ligament
A tough strap of connective tissue that holds bones together at joints.

microorganism
A living thing that can only be seen with a microscope.

molecule
A tiny particle made from two or more atoms.

nephron
One of the tiny filtration units in the kidneys that make urine.

neuron
A nerve cell that transmits electrical signals.

nutrient
A substance in food that provides cells with energy and materials for growth and repair.

organ
A body part made of tissues that has a specific role.

oxygen
A gas used by cells to release energy.

pathogen
A microorganism that causes disease.

protein
One of a group of substances that perform many roles, including as enzymes and antibodies.

skeletal muscle
A type of muscle that is attached to bones and moves the body.

smooth muscle
A type of muscle found in hollow organs that contracts slowly and rhythmically to move something.

sphincter
A ring of muscle that controls the flow of liquid through an opening.

system
A group of linked organs that work together to perform a specific role.

thermogram
An image that shows the amount of heat released by parts of the body.

tissue
A community of cells that work together.

vein
A blood vessel that carries blood toward the heart.

ventricle
One of two lower heart chambers.

X-ray
A technique that uses a form of radiation and photographic film to produce images of bones and other dense tissues.

Index

A page number in **bold** refers to the main entry for that subject

Acknowledgments

Dorling Kindersley would like to thank Chris Bernstein for the index.

Picture Credits
The publisher would like to thank the following for their kind permission to reproduce their photographs:

(Key: a-above; b-below/bottom; c-center; l-left; r-right; t-top)

Alamy Images: Scott Camazine 21cl; Kari Marttila 21br; Dennis Kunkel/PHOTOTAKE Inc. 68bl; DK Images: Geoff Brightling, courtesy of Denoyer-Geppert Intl. 42-43; Mary Evans Picture Library: 8-9; Science & Society Picture Library: 88l; Science Photo Library: 13cra, 23br, 46ca, 46cl, 54bc, 54bl,

80bl; Anatomical Travelogue 33b; Francis LeRoy, Biocosmos 44c; Kenneth Eward/Biografx 66t; Biophoto Associates 12cl; Dr. Arnold Brody 73t; BSIP 25t; BSIP Edwige 88tr; BSIP, Chassenet 36l; BSIP, Humbert/Amel. Magali 86b; CNRI 38bl, 49tc, 52bl, 53t, 70c, 89br; Brad Nelson/Custom Medical Stock Photo 53br; Richard Wehr/Custom Medical Stock Photo 84l; Robert Becker/Custom Medical Stock Photo 15cr; Gregory Dimijian 37br; Du Cane Medical Imaging Ltd 23bl; Brian Evans 55tr; Dr. Tim Evans 11tr; Eye of Science 49br, 56tl, 62tl, 85cr; Simon Fraser 50tr, 86-87c; GCa 19bl; David Gifford 26cb; GJLP 16cb, 33ca; GJLP/CNRI 89; Pascal Goetgheluck 68tl; Gustoimages 22c, 27clb; Adam Hart-Davis 78ca, 78t; Institut Paoli-Calmettes, ISM 28tl; Helene Fournie, ISM 55br; ISM 86t; Jean Abitbol, ISM 70bl, 70br; P. Sole, ISM 11br; Sovereign, ISM 41tl; Astrid Kage 65cr; Manfred Kage 47br, 55bl, 57br; Mehau Kulyk 32bc, 33cb, 89l; Lunagrafix 67br; David M. Martin, MD 59r, 62c, 63cr, 71cr; Miriam Maslo 27br; Tony McConnell 87b; Astrid & Hanns-Frieder Michler 58br; Hank Morgan 31br, 41br, 41crb; Don Fawcett 35b, 83t; Prof. P. Motta/Dept. of Anatomy/University "La Sapienza," Rome 42bl, 42br, 58tl, 63br, 64l, 65bl, 65tr; Professors P. Motta & T. Naguro 69c; Professors P.M. Motta, P.M. Andrews, K.R. Porter & J. Vial 81b; Steve Gschmeissner 12bl, 13bl, 13crb, 15tr, 30br, 34l, 38c, 39tl, 48c, 49cb, 52tr, 59bl, 62bl, 71tr, 82t; C. J. Guerin, PhD, MRC Toxicology Unit 31tr; National Cancer Institute 45cr; Susumu Nishinaga 15tl, 36c, 39br, 39tr, 43tr, 44b, 61bl, 64c, 69l, 85br; Omikron 37cr; Alfred Pasieka 18cl, 20bl, 28bl, 72bl, 88br; Ed Reschke/Peter Arnold Inc 55tl; Phantomotix 10cl; Philippe Plailly 46cb; Russell Kightley 11l; Dept. of Clinical Radiology, Salisbury District Hospital 21ca; David Scharf 85t; Dr. K. F. R. Schiller 60c; SCIMAT 56br; Dr. Gary Settles 74bl; Andrew Syred 14br; Arthur Toga/UCLA 33tl; Victor Habbick Visions 10cr; M. I. Walker 48b; Zephyr 17tl, 40b, 43tl, 67bl, 73cr, 74t

Historical images from the title "Medical and Anatomical Illustrations," edited by Jim Harter, courtesy of Dover Publications.

All other images © Dorling Kindersley
For further information see: www.dkimages.com

Every effort has been made to trace all copyright holders. The publishers will be pleased to hear from any copyright holders not here acknowledged.

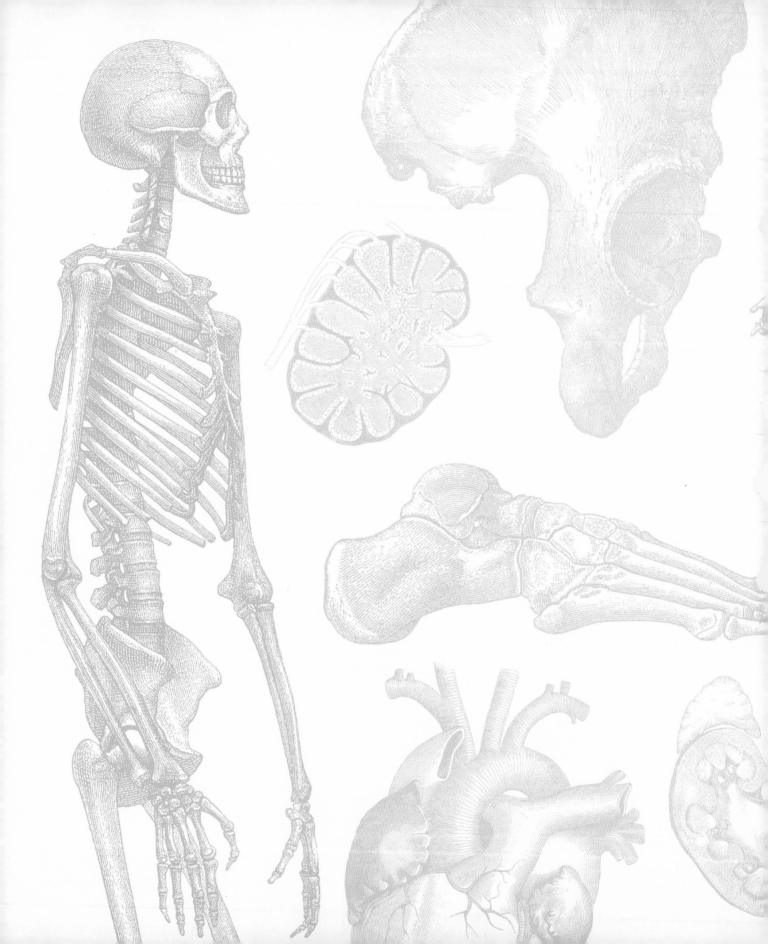

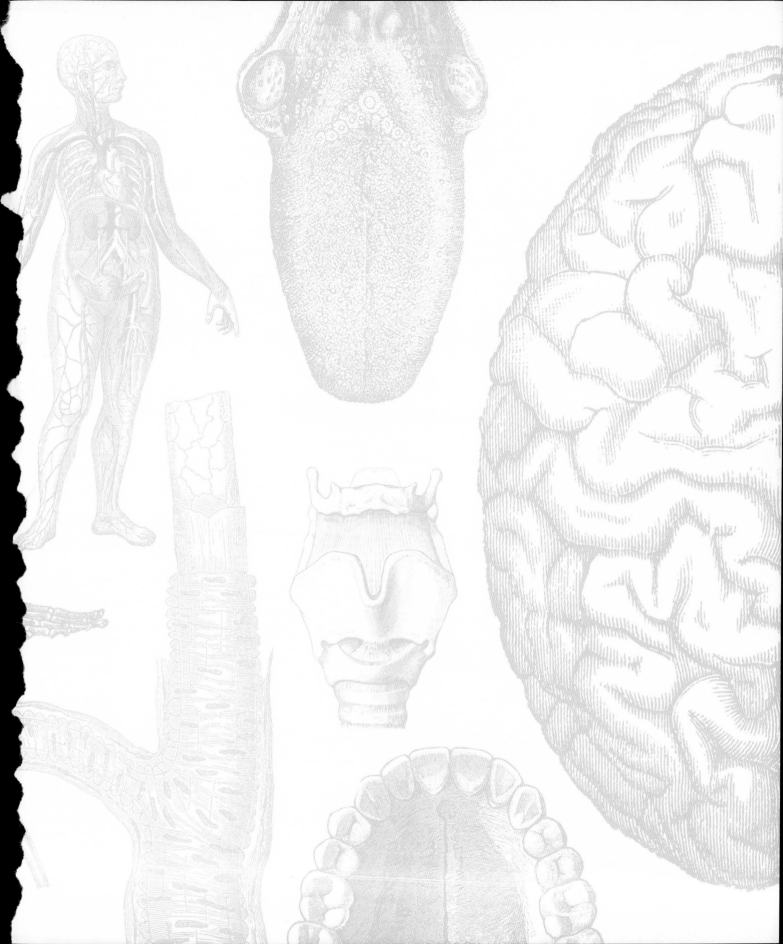